★ ★ ★

Jesse James Lived and Died in Texas

★ ★ ★

★   ★   ★

Jesse James
Lived and Died
in Texas

★   ★   ★

by
Betty Dorsett Duke

EAKIN PRESS ★ AUSTIN, TEXAS

I dedicate this book
with love and respect
to the voices of the past:

Jesse W. Dorsett,
Ida James Dorsett,
William James Dorsett,
and Jesse W. James.

Their presence is still felt.

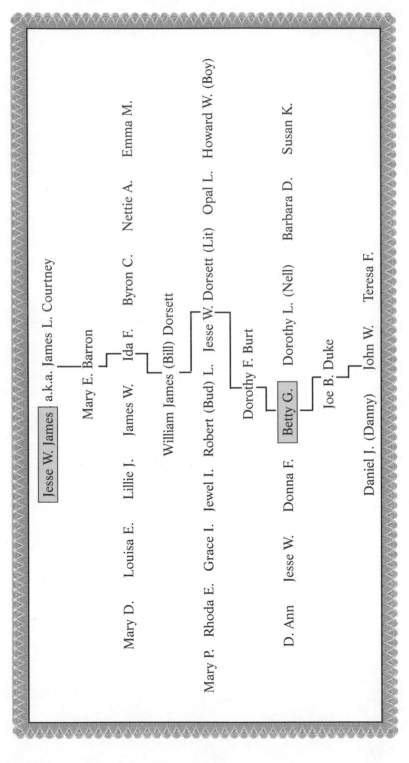

Author's family tree traced back to her great-grandfather, Jesse James.

★　　★　　★

Contents

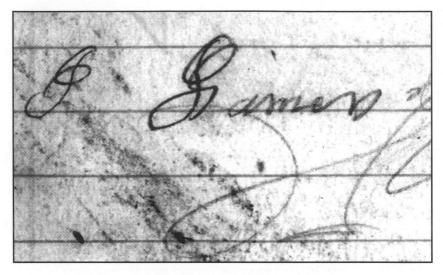

James L. Courtney signed a page of his diary "J. James."

* * *

Preface

Contrary to popular opinion, Jesse W. James wasn't shot dead by Bob Ford on April 3, 1882, and isn't buried in Missouri.

Many others before me have made this claim, but, unlike the rest, I have strong evidence that cannot be denied.

The comparisons between historically accepted James/ Samuel family photos and my family photos are remarkable. The photos speak for themselves.

Although the 1995 exhumation of the questioned grave in Kearney, Missouri, claims to have proven that Jesse was buried there and *has* succeeded in closing many people's minds to my claim, I have intriguing evidence to the contrary. After careful research I have my own conclusions about who is really buried in that grave.

This has been a complicated and confusing process for me, but worthwhile. If I hadn't heard the story about my great-grandfather's true identity all of my life, I would never have tried to solve the mystery of what really happened to America's most famous outlaw, Jesse James.

★ ★ ★

Acknowledgments

The author extends her thanks to the following individuals
and agencies for their invaluable help:

Joe B. Duke
Teresa F. Duke
Daniel J. Duke
Mr. and Mrs. John W. Duke
Dorothy Dorsett Nunn
Jesse Wayne Dorsett
Mr. and Mrs. Bill Dorsett
Mr. and Mrs. Arthur Leon Campbell
Ed Eakin
David Baskin, Texas State Library and Archives
William McCann,
Austin Police Department's Forensic Multi-Media Lab
Texas Department of Public Safety
Megan G. Tormey and Dr. Joseph J. Atick,
Visionics Corporation
Falls County Courthouse
Bell County Courthouse
McLennan County Courthouse
Texas Ranger Hall of Fame, Waco, Texas
Mary Beck, Missouri State Archives, Jefferson City
Dr. William Savage, University of Oklahoma

★ ★ ★

Introduction

After debating for more than two years about whether to go public about my great-grandfather's true identity, my family and I decided that the true story about the fate of Jesse James should be known.

In 1997 I contacted *Texas Monthly* magazine and spoke to John Broders, telling him that I had a story that I thought they would be interested in. When he asked what the story was, I told him that Jesse James was my great-grandfather and that he wasn't killed in 1882 but faked his death and lived to be an old man and died in Texas. At the other end of the telephone line there was complete silence. I knew he thought I was insane, but thankfully he was polite enough to listen to my story. He asked me to mail copies of some photograph comparisons I had. After receiving them, he called and said that either I was the best con artist of the twentieth century or I was telling the truth.

I had received the same reaction from everyone who had seen the photograph comparisons of my ancestors to known photos of the James/Samuel family. (Jesse James' mother married Dr. Samuel after the death of Jesse's father.) I was pretty naive about what a sensitive subject Jesse James is to some people, so I wasn't prepared for the negative reactions that were in store for me—especially from people who have a financial stake in keeping the Jesse James story just the way it has been for more than a hundred years.

I excitedly wrote to the modern-day James-Younger Gang to tell them my news. This organization's objective is "dedicated to the continued research and preservation of the history of the James and Younger families and the understanding of their lives and times." I thought they would be happy to know that Jesse had not been shot in the back of the head by one of his friends. I even included copies of my great-great-grandmother's photo and a historically known photo of Zerelda James Samuel (Jesse James' mother), both of which had been compared by a highly sensitive computer at the Texas Department of Public Safety, which showed that the gowns worn by the women in both photos were identical and that the women appeared to be the same person as well.

Well, I couldn't have been more mistaken about their reaction. I still have not heard from them.

I decided to mail the photo comparison of my great-great-grandmother and the known photo of Zerelda along with a letter outlining my claim to the James Farm in Kearney, Missouri. After a few weeks of not getting a response, I decided to contact them to see what they thought. I was referred to Beth Beckett, and after confirming that they had received the material, I asked her what they thought of the photo comparison. She really surprised me by saying that no one there thought the women looked alike and that the dresses did not appear to be identical.

It seemed as though I had run into a brick wall.

After thinking things over, I decided to contact someone in Missouri who was knowledgeable about the James/Samuel family and who wouldn't have any reason for concealing a true opinion. The person who came to mind was Jack Wymore, owner of the building that was the site of the first bank robbery by the James Gang. Wymore's ancestors owned the building at the time of the holdup and one of them was shot and killed by a gang member during the getaway. I contacted Wymore by telephone and he sounded very interested. I overnighted the photo comparison and other material to him and eagerly awaited his response. There was none. When I called him back a few days later, he informed me that the two women looked nothing alike and that the dresses weren't similar at all.

I couldn't believe what I was hearing. It turns out that Wymore leases the old bank building-turned-museum to the Clay

County Parks Department. He also has a large and what he believes to be authentic collection of James/Samuel family photos. Of course, some of those very photos will be proven false in light of my claim.

The closest thing I've had to an affirmation of my family photos from Missouri came from a reporter at the *Liberty Tribune*. After seeing known photos of Zerelda James/Samuel and Jesse James compared to my old family photos, she came up with the theory that Jesse James had to be a bigamist! My great-grandfather had married Mary Ellen Barron in 1871 and had eight children in Texas. History reports that Jesse married Zee Mimms in 1874. He would have been an extremely busy man, running back and forth from Texas to Missouri by horseback or train.

One magazine editor who focuses on the Old West period suggested that I just drop my entire claim even if I am right. He said that he didn't think I realized that there are people who will dedicate their lives to discrediting me.

I was in a predicament. I needed someone who was considered an expert in facial identification to examine my photographs in order to lend credibility to my claim.

An internationally noted forensic artist at the Texas Department of Public Safety examined and compared my family photos to known photos of the James/Samuel family and was very impressed, but would not allow me to publish her name.

I contacted the American Academy of Forensic Science in Colorado and they suggested that I contact a local crime lab. I took their advice and called the Austin Police Department. William S. McCann, supervisor of the forensic multi-media lab, agreed to see me and said he would like to have some other people take a look at my photographs.

McCann, Mark Gillespie (director of the forensic sciences division), and Cathy Wallace (police photographer) all visually examined the photographs (in a non-technical way) and were very impressed with what they saw. They believe my family photos match the known photos of the James/Samuel family.

Even though the above experts believed that my family photographs match historically accepted photographs of Jesse James and many members of his family, I still needed a computer-analyzed match of the two sets of photographs to lend credence to my claim.

The American Academy of Forensic Science gave me the names of several experts in photograph comparisons. Dr. James Ibert was listed, so I contacted him. He referred me to Visionics Corporation, world leaders in face recognition technology, and they graciously agreed to view my photographs.

After examining both sets of photographs, I received this official statement of recognition: "Dr. Joseph J. Atick and Megan G. Tormey from Visionics Corporation examined the photographs through computerized matching, analytical as well as visual inspection techniques. They concluded with reasonable confidence that the faces in question matched each other and belonged to the same individual."

I have always admired people who have the courage to speak the truth, especially since this is such a controversial subject. I will always be grateful to them.

If I had only one family photograph that matched a member of the James/Samuel family, I wouldn't have much on which to base my claim. But there are numerous family photos that match known photos of the James/Samuel family.

Along with the photographs, I have other strong evidence, such as census records, oral and written family history, historical documents proving a Courtney (my family; his alias) connection to the James/Samuel family, and my great-grandfather's diary, which he signed "J. James."

The people who are disputing my claim are probably hoping that I will eventually give up my pursuit. But I'm like Capt. Leander McNelly, an early-day Texas Ranger, who said, "No man in the wrong can stand up against a man in the right who keeps on-a-comin'."

Chapter 1

★ ★ ★

Jesse's Early Years

*A*fter more than a century, the truth about what really happened to Jesse James has come to light.

Many people have questioned the historically accepted story that Jesse was shot dead on April 3, 1882, by Bob Ford. Now there is much more evidence pointing to the fact that Jesse got by with his own murder and lived to be an old man.

The real James descendants, or so they say, had the body that was buried in Kearney, Missouri, under the name Jesse Woodson James exhumed in 1995 for DNA testing to "silence anyone claiming some relation to the famous outlaw Jesse James once and for all."

False claimants may be silenced, but the true descendants of Jesse James won't be.

I have strong evidence that Jesse W. James lived more than seventy years of his life in Texas and is buried in Texas soil.

It's been said that Jesse James' name is one of the three most famous names in the world, but many people only know that he robbed banks and trains. They don't know about the events that led to his becoming an outlaw and a legend known worldwide. I am starting at the beginning of his life, so that maybe by the end of my story you will understand what drove him to take the actions that he did, and you will finally know the truth about what really happened to Jesse James.

1

Robert Sallee James married Zerelda Elizabeth Cole on December 28, 1841, in Kentucky. In 1842 the Jameses moved to Clay County in Missouri, and settled on a 275-acre farm outside of the small town of Kearney, which was then known as Centerville. Robert was an ordained Baptist preacher, earning his master of arts degree at Georgetown College in 1847. He became the pastor of New Hope Baptist Church, located not far from their farm in Kearney, and helped organize the William Jewel College in Liberty, Missouri. The Jameses became a very prosperous and respected family.

Robert and Zerelda had four children: Alexander Franklin James (b. January 19, 1843); Robert R. James (b. July 19, 1845, d. August 21, 1845); Jesse Woodson James (b. September 5, 1847); and Susan Lavenia James (b. November 25, 1849).

Robert was away from home much of the time in his duties with the church, which left Zerelda in a position where she had to take charge of the farm. That probably wasn't a problem for her, because she was a proud, intelligent woman with a mind of her own.

The James family lived in the part of Missouri known as "The Border Region." They had black slaves, as did many of the wealthier families in Clay County, to help with the farm. Slaveholding was a normal way of life for most of the whites in Missouri. A majority of them had originally come from farther south, where owning slaves was common. In fact, Missouri's first state constitution contained a clause that required free blacks to stay out of the state.

In 1850 Robert James left his family for the gold rush to California. There are many theories as to why he went. Some say there was trouble in his marriage; others say he had gold fever. I don't believe any living person can say why he went, but he wasn't in California very long when he became ill and died on August 18, 1850, at the age of thirty-two. He is believed to be buried in an unmarked grave.

Strong-willed Zerelda was now a widow, and she became the influencing force in the lives of Frank and Jesse James.

On September 30, 1852, Zerelda married Benjamin Simms. It was a short marriage. Some have claimed that Simms mistreated Frank and Jesse and that the protective Zerelda would not tolerate it. The couple were in the process of getting a divorce when Simms was killed in a horse accident.

As the old saying goes, the third time must have been a charm for Zerelda. On September 26, 1855, she married Dr. Reuben Samuel, a quiet, steady family man who spent a lot of time with the family and treated her children like his own. Zerelda and Dr. Samuel had four more children of their own: Archie, John, Fannie, and Sarah Louisa (Sallie).

Like most country boys, Frank and Jesse learned to ride horses and shoot. This was something that would help them tremendously later on in life. They also learned all there was to know about the surrounding countryside. The boys knew where every deer trail, road, and river crossing was located. This, too, was something that would help them tremendously later on in life. They were known for having no fear and seemed to have inherited this trait from their mother, who had maintained her reputation of being intelligent, courageous, and fearless.

In general, Jesse and Frank's childhood was normal. Their mother ran the house and Dr. Samuel and the boys took charge of the farming. But soon the winds of change blew into Missouri—and throughout the country.

Chapter 2

★　　★　　★

Troubled Times

T ENSIONS BEGAN TO BUILD over slavery in the 1850s. Most of the immigrants coming into Missouri were from Germany and Ireland and opposed slavery. New settlers from the northern regions of the country shared the immigrants' view.

Many of the Southerners in Missouri resented the Northerners and foreigners and considered them a threat to their way of life. Rioting began to break out between the pro- and anti-slavery partisans.

For years before the Civil War became official, tensions between Kansas and Missouri were building. Jayhawkers, as those from the anti-slavery Kansas side were called, along with the Red-Legs (Union abolitionist guerrillas), had started slave-stealing raids in Missouri, burning farms and looting. Often the slaves freed during those raids would end up being sold back to their original owners, turning a nice profit for the abolitionists. Slave-owners, deciding to take matters into their own hands, formed gangs, such as the Blue Lodges and Kickapoo Rangers, and rode into Kansas to seek revenge on the abolitionists. They burned farms, ambushed settlers, and voted illegally in elections, putting Kansas in control of pro-slavery officials. Men from both sides of the border burned, looted, and murdered.

The tensions were felt nationwide. South Carolina was the

4

first to secede from the Union in 1860, followed by Mississippi, Florida, Alabama, Georgia, and Louisiana. In 1861 there were more secessions: Texas, Virginia, Arkansas, North Carolina, and Tennessee.

Missouri's legislators called a special session to decide whether to join the Confederacy, but when the votes were counted, Missouri was still in the Union. Missouri was stuck between a rock and a hard place. Their leaders' support for the Union ran deep, but most of Missouri's citizens supported the South.

The citizens of Missouri had different opinions from the delegates who supported Abe Lincoln's administration. Missouri men who considered themselves Unionists found it difficult to be loyal when the Kansas raiders had just stolen all their livestock and personal belongings and then burned their homes to the ground.

When Confederate artillerymen began bombarding army post Fort Sumter, the war became official. The date was April 12, 1861.

Missouri's Governor Clairborne Fox Jackson rejected the U.S. secretary of war's request for the remaining Union states to raise troops to fight the Confederate Rebels. After a futile attempt to declare that Missouri be seceded from the Union and join the Confederacy, Governor Jackson, along with a few legislators, left St. Louis and fled to the Arkansas border.

Sterling Price, Governor Jackson's brother-in-law, was placed in command of Jackson's state guard. The Union army wanted Missouri on their side and so did the Rebels. The Union army commander asked Washington for more ammunition and men.

In Liberty, Missouri, Southern supporters captured a Federal arsenal and came away with cannons and small firearms. Frank James joined the Home Guard that sided with the South. In April of 1862, the provisional state government of Missouri offered amnesty for ex-Confederate soldiers. Frank signed the papers and took the oath of allegiance to the United States of America. Several months later, the provisional government ordered all adult men to enlist in the state militia so they could fight for the Union. That's when Frank went to the bush and joined William Clark Quantrill's Confederate Partisan Rangers (commonly referred to as guerrillas).

The Partisan Rangers were a legitimate part of the Confederate military. The Rangers were armed with Colt six-shooters, and had fine, fast horses. They knew the terrain they rode over as well as they knew the backs of their hands. During the day, Missouri was under the control of Federal troops, but the tables were turned at night. Yankees soon learned they were no match for the Rebs in the bush and hollows.

A Missouri militia regiment rode to the Samuel farm in the spring of 1863, looking for Frank and the Rangers he rode with. The Samuels and Jesse were accused of being spies. The Union troops claimed the Samuels were giving supplies and information to Quantrill and his men.

The militiamen grabbed Dr. Samuel and tried to force information about the whereabouts of Quantrill and his men from him; when he refused, they hanged him by the neck from a tree. They would let him hang awhile, then lower him. This was repeated several times. Dr. Samuel bravely kept silent about Frank's location, until the militia finally gave up and left him hanging. They then found Zerelda, who was pregnant, and tried to make her tell them where they could find Quantrill and his men. When she refused, they threw her across the room into a wall.

Jesse was plowing a field when the militia found him. Surrounding him, they demanded to know where they could find Frank. When they realized he would not cooperate, he was severely beaten. Somehow he managed to get back to the house, where he found his mother trying to revive her husband. Even though Zerelda had managed to cut the rope, saving Dr. Samuel's life, he suffered brain damage from the incident which resulted in him having to be institutionalized later on in life.

Dr. Samuel was a man to admire. He risked his life trying to protect Frank, proving his love for Zerelda and her children that day.

The militiamen left and promised worse punishment on their next visit, and a few weeks later they lived up to that promise. Zerelda was arrested, and along with her youngest children, was jailed. They were starved and mistreated.

In July of 1863, Dr. Samuel was jailed by the provost marshal in Liberty, Missouri. Some of the Samuels' neighbors banded together and signed an affidavit trying to obtain his release from jail. The neighbors were A. C. Courtney, L. W. Lunkin, and Alvah Maret.

Blinded by hate and seeking retaliation, Jesse tried to join Quantrill and fight alongside Frank. Quantrill thought Jesse was too young, so Jesse sought out Bill Anderson and was allowed to join. Anderson was greatly feared; it has been said his main goal in life was to kill Yankees. His father and one of his sisters had been killed by the militia, and Anderson was consumed with fury.

Gen. Thomas C. Ewing, Jr., a commander of the Union army in Kansas City, had ordered all female relatives of Quantrill's Partisan Rangers to be arrested. The women had been detained in a three-story building in Kansas. The building collapsed. Some believe Union troops had pulled the supports out from under it on purpose, killing several women and severely injuring others. Bill Anderson's sister was one of the women killed in the collapsed building.

Quantrill and Anderson retaliated. A message was sent out for men who had ridden with them in the past to gather in Johnson County, Missouri. About five hundred men responded.

Cole Younger led the unit that Frank James was in to Johnson County. Kansas Jayhawkers had murdered Cole's father after looting and burning their farm. He, too, joined the Bushwackers of Missouri to get revenge.

Quantrill told his fellow Rangers that he planned to destroy Lawrence, Kansas.

Most of Quantrill's men were armed with at least six revolvers, so that if one revolver ran out of ammunition during a battle they wouldn't have to take valuable time to reload. They also carried Bowie knives and shotguns.

They wore homespun embroidered woolen shirts, and they were riding the best horses on the border. Some of the men wore Union uniforms that they took off dead Yankees. The uniforms came in handy when the Rangers tricked Union troops with surprise attacks, or when the men were hungry and needed a home-cooked meal made by a Union farmer's wife.

The order was given for many men in Lawrence to be killed and the buildings burned. With the wild Rebel yell, the Bush-wackers started destroying the town early on the morning of August 21, 1863. Men were killed in front of their families, and homes and businesses were burned. Bill Anderson killed with a vengeance, remembering the deaths of his family. This was the day he started to be called "Bloody Bill."

Between one hundred and fifty and two hundred males were killed at Lawrence. Frank James was said to be there, but it's believed that Jesse wasn't part of the attack.

Union General Ewing struck back by ordering all people living in Jackson, Cass, Bates, and half of Vernon counties (all on the Kansas border) to leave their homes. This was General Order Number Eleven. Thousands of people in Missouri left their homes in fear. Union soldiers marched through the area destroying everything. They destroyed so completely, it became known as the "Burnt District."

The state government would no longer offer amnesty to Partisan Rangers, as it had in 1862 to Frank James. The Rangers responded by offering no paroles to their prisoners. In the past, they would let them go free if they promised not to fight again. The Black Flag Era had come to Missouri, promising no surrender and no prisoners.

The Bushwackers (Partisan Rangers) rode to Sherman, Texas, spending the winter there. A dispute arose between Quantrill and Anderson, causing Anderson and his men to leave and set up their own camp.

Frank remained with Quantrill and during that time met Gen. Joseph Shelby and his adjutant, Maj. John Newman Edwards. - Edwards, a former newspaperman, helped Frank and Jesse immensely later on. Shelby had led raids on Kansas before the war and was now a cavalry officer. Because of the admiration Shelby and Edwards had for Frank and Jesse James, they formed a lasting friendship.

Jesse was only sixteen years old but caught on quickly to the ways of the Bushwackers. He could ride a horse like the wind. Placing the reins in his mouth, and holding a six-shooter in each hand, he could hit his target dead on, barely taking time to aim. Bloody Bill praised Jesse by saying "not to have any beard, he is the cleanest and keenest fighter in the command" (J. N. Edwards, *Noted Guerrillas*, p. 176). The fact that Jesse had no fear made him an ominous opponent in battle.

John N. Edwards (in *Noted Guerrillas*, 203) reported that

Jesse and another young Ranger, James Hinds, "in there boyish wantoness, would pick the hottest and most dangerous positions during a battle, laughing always and always where the most killing was."

History reports that Jesse was nicknamed "Dingus" by his companions. There are several accounts of how this came about:

- Jesse and the Partisan Rangers were sitting around a campfire one night, and Jesse was cleaning his pistol when it went off, taking off the tip of the middle finger on his left hand.
- Another story is that Jesse was part of a fight in Clay County, killing two Union men from the Bigelow family. He supposedly shot off the tip of his middle finger during the fight.
- Still another story has it that a horse was the culprit, having bitten off the tip of Jesse's finger.

In all accounts, he is supposed to have yelled out in pain, "Dingus!" He was supposedly called Dingus for the rest of the war. Whether or not Jesse was actually missing one of his fingers remains a mystery.

Frank was given the nickname "Buck," the origin of which is unknown. He had the reputation of being a good scout, something that required calm nerves and paying close attention to details.

"Bloody Bill" Anderson ordered his men to Centralia, Missouri. Anderson, Jesse, and the rest of the Rangers attacked the town. Following Anderson's orders, the men piled railroad ties on the tracks to stop any trains coming into town. A train from St. Charles pulled in, stopping at the pile of ties. There were Union soldiers on board. Anderson ordered the men stripped of their uniforms; then the men were shot and scalped.

Upon seeing the massacre at Centralia, Maj. A.V.E. Johnson went after the Bushwackers, swearing to kill every one of them. When the two forces met, Anderson ordered his men into a line facing the mounted infantry of the state militia. With the two opposing sides facing each other, the Rangers were ordered to dismount and cinch up their horses' saddle girths before the battle. Major Johnson's infantry dismounted, thinking they were going to fight on foot, and every fourth man led away the other horses. When the infantry's horses were off the field, the Rangers jumped back on their horses and charged. Jesse led the charge killing the major, an act which reportedly led to an indictment after the war. The Bushwackers were victorious that day.

Gen. Sterling Price convinced the leaders of the Confederacy that he could take Missouri from Union control. His army was badly equipped and slow-moving as they marched north for St. Louis. Price encountered Union General Ewing at Pilot Knob Hill and decided to attack, ignoring Shelby's objections. It was a mistake, because more than a thousand Confederate troops were killed. Price then realized he couldn't retake St. Louis and headed for Kansas City.

Several weeks after the battles of Pilot Knob and Centralia, Anderson's Partisan Rangers rode into Price's camp to join forces with the Confederate troops. Jesse James and the other Rangers were in good shape compared to Price's tattered soldiers.

Shelby led his Iron Brigade and the Partisan Rangers, including Frank and Jesse James. They attacked a Union force in Lexington, pushing them out of the city. They were also successful in other skirmishes in the area, but the Union sent reinforcements that soon caught the Confederates under General Price, who was moving too slowly.

The Confederates were defeated. Soon after the battle, Bloody Bill Anderson was claimed to have been killed along with other Rangers. Jesse James, Archie Clement, and a few others escaped and continued to fight in Arkansas. Quantrill was also claimed to have been killed in Kentucky, shot by Captain Terrill and his men. Frank James and others survived and surrendered to the Union forces on July 26, 1865.

Jesse and some of his companions raised a white flag of surrender and were riding along a road to Lexington, Missouri, when Union soldiers opened fire on them. Jesse is said to have been shot in the chest, and his horse killed. The Bushwackers scattered, firing back at the Yankees as they rode away. When Jesse crawled into some brush, a couple of the Union soldiers saw him and followed, trying to kill him. Jesse fired on them, killing one of their horses. The two Yankees gave up the fight and retreated to safety. Jesse was badly wounded and spent a feverish, painful night near a creek. The next morning a farmer found him and took him to a doctor.

The Civil War was over, but if you were from Missouri and

★ ★ ★

*In 1865 Missouri adopted the Drake
Constitution which prohibited Confederate
soldiers and sympathizers from practicing
many professions, preaching the gospel, or
being deacons in their churches. Amnesty
was granted to Union soldiers for their
acts after January 1, 1861, resulting in
Missouri being overrun with carpetbag
public officials, many of whom came from
Kansas.*

★ ★ ★

happened to be an ex-Confederate or Ranger, you were treated like a second-class citizen. Laws were passed that clearly discriminated against former Confederates.

A law passed by the Missouri provisional government's Constitution of 1865 granted amnesty to Union soldiers found guilty of breaking any law after January 1, 1861, "in military service of the United States or the state, or in pursuance of orders issued by state, or National military officials." This pardon did not apply to ex-Confederate Partisan Rangers; acts they committed during the war were held against them. They couldn't hold office, vote, practice certain professions, or serve as deacons in their churches. As the saying goes, "To the victor go the spoils."

The Samuels had returned to their farm as soon as they could after the war, but money was scarce. The county governments were controlled by radical Republicans who sold abandoned farms to people from Northern states.

Clay County was still inhabited by a majority of Southern sympathizers, and citizens there formed mobs to stand up to the Radical Republicans. They threatened officials, causing the governor to send in the state militia. The militiamen robbed and murdered the residents of Clay County, doing more harm than good, so the people asked for protection from Federal troops. Three companies of U.S. Army troops came to their defense and kicked the militia out. It seems that an unofficial war was still being fought.

When any group of people is being oppressed, there are always a few who will rise up and strike back at their oppressors. Two brothers named James were among the few who would strike back. The events experienced by them during and after the Civil War had led to the formation of the James Gang, and they would become the most famous outlaws in American history.

Chapter 3

★ ★ ★

The Making of a Legend

RANK AND JESSE JAMES, the Younger brothers—Cole, John, Bob, and Jim—and many other ex-Confederate Partisan Rangers, made up the gang. At times there would be as many as twelve men riding together, and at other times only a few.

On February 13, 1866, the Clay County Savings Bank in Liberty, Missouri, was robbed of $62,000. Ten to twelve men wearing blue Union coats rode into Liberty. Two of the men went into the bank and asked the cashier to change a large bill. The men didn't really need change; they actually wanted all of the bank's money. They held their pistols on the cashier and filled a large grain sack with gold, silver, paper currency, and bearer bonds. It is not known if Frank and Jesse were present at the robbery, but several of their former Bushwacker friends were identified. Bill and James Wilkerson were two members of the gang known to be there.

Alexander, Mitchell and Company Bank was robbed next in Lexington, Missouri, on October 30, 1866. A tall, friendly man asked the cashier to cash a bond. As the cashier was explaining that the bank didn't buy that type of bond, two or more armed men walked in. A total of $2,000 was put into the grain sack, and since the cashier would not give them the key to the vault, they left. A posse led by ex-Confederate Rangers John and David Pool was organized to chase the desperadoes, but they gave up after a short chase and returned home.

About a dozen of Frank James' old Ranger comrades gathered to plan the next robbery. Cole Younger, Andy McGuire, Payne Jones, Thomas Little, and Allen Parmer were said to be present.

The next bank hit was the Hughes and Wasson bank in Richmond, east of Clay County, on May 22, 1867. The outlaws collected about $4,000 in their grain sack. Seeing so many armed men on horseback waiting outside the bank, the local men became suspicious. A gunfight took place, killing some of Richmond's citizens. Lawmen later captured Thomas Little and Andy McGuire and threw them in jail. Angry lynch mobs broke into the jail and hanged them both.

Frank and Jesse James, Oliver and George Shepherd, Cole Younger, and other members of the gang robbed Nimrod Long's Bank in Russelville, Kentucky, taking about $14,000. Mr. Long hired a detective from Louisville by the name of D. G. Bligh, and he notified lawmen in Jackson County, Missouri, of the results of his investigation. The lawmen shot Oliver Shepherd at his farm and tracked down his brother George. George served a three-year prison term for his part in the holdup. Frank, Jesse, and Cole were suspects but were never arrested.

Having a commanding presence and fearing nothing, Jesse James soon became the gang's leader. Different men would ride in the raids, but the James boys and Younger brothers were the main members. They pretended to be cattle buyers, wearing long dusters that helped conceal most of the weapons with which they armed themselves.

It was the Gallatin, Missouri, holdup on December 7, 1869, that made the James name hit the newspaper. John W. Sheets, a Union officer who had been in the battle when Bloody Bill Anderson was said to have been shot dead, was the owner of the Davies County Savings Bank. It is believed that Frank James went to the counter and asked Sheets to change a $100 bill. Jesse is reported to have asked Sheets to write out a receipt. As Sheets was writing the receipt, Jesse is claimed to have shot him in the head, killing him. A bank clerk by the name of McDowell told reporters that the gunman had said that Sheets and Cox killed his brother. Jesse thought of Bill Anderson as a brother, and had sworn revenge on his killers, or so historians say.

(I have suspicions, which I cannot prove, that Anderson wasn't killed as history reported. One day I was looking at the other tombstones in Blevins Cemetery, where my great-grandfather is buried, when I noticed one that bore the name William Anderson. That immediately caught my attention because of the connection between Jesse James and Bill Anderson. They are said to have been like brothers. History reports that some of the Partisan Rangers went to Kentucky after Anderson was claimed to have been killed in the assault by Union Maj. S. P. Cox in 1864.

The William Anderson buried in Blevins Cemetery moved to Texas from Kentucky in 1873, two years after my great-grandfather arrived, and what I find extremely intriguing is that the date of birth on Anderson's tombstone is October 31, 1846—the exact same birthdate that is inscribed on my great-grandfather's tombstone. I believe October 31, 1846, is a fake birthdate given by my great-grandfather and William Anderson, and that it may have had some significance known only by the Partisan Rangers.

My father's sister, Irene, wrote that my great-grandfather had been a Ranger. It was assumed that she meant a Texas Ranger when I first began my research. But after checking records I learned that he wasn't a Texas Ranger; he was a Partisan Ranger.)

As the gang was making their getaway after the Gallatin hold-up, Jesse's horse spooked, throwing him off the saddle. His foot became hung in the stirrup and Jesse was dragged for a short distance. Finally freeing his foot, Jesse jumped up behind Frank and they raced away, leaving his horse.

The fine horse that was left behind was identified by the sheriff as one belonging to Jesse James, who lived in Clay County. The sheriff went to the James farm to arrest the James boys. A young slave ran and warned Frank and Jesse that the sheriff was coming, allowing them to escape. They were never arrested.

The citizens of Clay County stood behind their friends, Frank and Jesse. They hated the Radical Republican government and the railroads that were in control of Missouri, so they provided alibis and hideouts for the James boys.

Knowing the country thoroughly and having so many friends, not only in Missouri but also Kentucky, Arkansas, New Mexico, Colorado, and Texas, the James brothers escaped capture. Even

★   ★   ★

Donnie Pence, member of the James Gang, later became a sheriff in Kentucky. According to The Story of Cole Younger, *Jim, Cole's brother, was a deputy sheriff of Dallas County in 1870 and 1871.*

★   ★   ★

though they had exceptional abilities with pistols and horses, Frank and Jesse James also possessed a tremendous amount of luck.

The James Gang decided to go north to Iowa on June 3, 1871. Clell Miller, Cole Younger, Frank and Jesse robbed the bank in Corydon. On the way out of town, they noticed a group of people listening to a politician giving a speech. Jesse liked to joke around and interrupted the speech, telling the crowd that the bank had just been robbed. People in the crowd yelled for him to keep quiet so the speech could continue. It was quite awhile before they discovered the bank really had been robbed.

It wasn't long before the James Gang decided to deal out a little justice to the railroads they hated so much. When Missouri was under radical rule the county governments issued nearly $19 million in bonds to finance the railroads. Most of Missouri's citizens had voted against issuing the bonds, but Republican county judges approved the bonds anyway, going against the vote of the people. The railroads bought up land and charged high shipping rates. The farmers were in debt from having to buy new farming equipment that was destroyed during the Civil War, and they couldn't afford to pay high shipping rates, plus property taxes that had been raised by the local government to pay the interest on the railroad bonds.

When the James Gang robbed the railroads, many people cheered them on. The taxpayers were revolting against the railroads and government. Lynch mobs and secret organizations were formed that encouraged people not to pay their taxes. The James Gang gave some of the holdup money to friends, neighbors, and relatives to help pay their debts.

The gang robbed the Chicago, Rock Island and Pacific Railroad on the night of July 21, 1873. They pulled a portion of the train rails out of line, which caused the engine to turn over, killing the engineer. Some have claimed that the gang thought the train would just stop.

On January 31, 1874, the gang robbed a train at Gads Hill, approximately 100 miles south of St. Louis. It was headed for Little Rock, Arkansas. They only robbed from the wealthy passengers and would not take money from men who had to work hard for a living. They would check a man's hands to see if he had calluses; if he did he was allowed to keep his valuables. Women on board were charmed by the good-looking, adventurous desperadoes.

The railroad companies were growing desperate and hired the Pinkerton National Detective Agency, formerly called the Pinkerton Government Guard. The Pinkertons were spies for the Union during the Civil War. Allen Pinkerton headed the agency, and his sons were employees.

A Pinkerton detective by the name of John Whicher was sent to the James farm in 1874, pretending to be a farm hand. He ignored warnings from a former sheriff that it was a foolish plan because Zerelda Samuel was a dangerous woman, and she would be as much of a threat as Frank and Jesse. She would protect her family at all costs. Whicher lodged at a boardinghouse in Liberty owned by another former sheriff of Clay County, W. J. Courtney. Courtney was the proprietor of the Arthur House at Liberty, Missouri, and served Whicher his last meal on earth. Unknown to Whicher, Courtney was a friend of the James/Samuel family.

The current sheriff of Clay County learned of the Pinkertons' plan and rode to the Samuel farm to warn his friends. Whicher's body was found the next day in Jackson County.

When the Pinkertons tried to capture the Youngers a few days later, a gunfight took place on the road and John Younger was killed.

By 1874, Missouri had gained the reputation of being an outlaw state. People from other states couldn't understand why the James Gang had never been captured. When election time rolled around, the issue of the gang was a top priority. The governor had tried to capture the gang, and he, too, was growing desperate. He asked legislators for $10,000 to hire a group of secret agents to try to bring them in. He also tried to get a special bill passed to have the state militia reactivated to aid in the capture.

Many of the Democratic legislators had fought for the Confederacy and sympathized with the James Gang. Although the legislators approved the request for the special fund, they denied the militia bill and one-third of the group refused to vote on the secret agent fund.

John Newman Edwards helped the James Gang to keep their good public image and also cast confusion about the gang by publicly upholding them in his newspaper. Zerelda Samuel was sent to a Democratic newspaper, *The Caucasian,* to report that her boys had been living in Mexico and had not committed the crimes for which they were accused. She said she could not have finer sons than Frank and Jesse James.

The newspaper described Zerelda as a "tall, dignified lady, of about forty eight years; graceful in carriage and gesture; calm and quiet in demeanor, with a ripple of fire now and then breaking through the placid surface, and of far more than ordinary intelligence and culture."

Around the same time, Cole Younger, adding to the confusion, had a letter published in a newspaper stating that he hated Jesse James and had not spoken to him for years. This really confused people. How could the James Gang be operating when two of the main leaders hated each other?

It was almost impossible to catch the James boys because there were no photographs or descriptions of them, and they had many friends to hide them out and provide alibis.

The pressure was on the Pinkertons to stop the gang. They sent an agent by the name of Jack Ladd to work on a neighboring farm owned by Daniel Askew. His job was to spy on the Samuel family. In January of 1875, Ladd sent a coded telegram to the Pinkertons stating that Jesse and Frank were at the family farm. The Pinkertons, thinking they finally had a break, sent a group of detectives to Kearney by a special train.

The men surrounded the James house around midnight on January 26, 1875, and threw a large ball of ignited turpentine-soaked cotton through the window, awakening the family. While the family and servants were trying to put out the fire that had started in the house, the Pinkertons were trying to set the outside of the house on fire. A short time later, the Pinkertons threw a round metal canister filled with kerosene through the window. Dr. Samuel and Zerelda tried to push the bomb into the fireplace with a tobacco stick but had to get a shovel to move it. They managed to push the canister into the fireplace, and just as they did it exploded. The explosion was so powerful it threw Dr. Samuel against the ceiling. Zerelda's right arm was so severely shattered it had to be amputated just below the elbow later that night. The Samuels' nine-year-old son Archie was in agony all night and died hours later. Dr. Samuel had serious cuts, possibly on one of his hands. This may explain why he had to call for another doctor to perform the surgery on Zerelda's arm. One of his hands appears to be deformed in family photographs of him.

This tragedy happened for nothing, because Pinkerton man Jack Ladd had been dead wrong. Frank and Jesse were not at the James/Samuel farm. If Frank and Jesse had been at their mother's home, more than likely the Pinkertons and their group of men would have died then and there.

The Pinkertons claimed that the bomb was thrown through the window to illuminate the room so they could see who was there, but in 1991, 116 years after the bombing incident took place, evidence was found by Ted Yatesman in the Library of Congress manuscript section that proved they were lying. Yatesman discovered a letter written by Allen Pinkerton to Samuel Hardwick, an attorney in Liberty, Missouri. Pinkerton told Hardwick "above everything destroy the house," and then later he wrote "burn the house down," to emphasize the first statement.

One of the Pinkerton detectives dropped his revolver in the Samuel yard in the panic of trying to get away. It was found the following day and was stamped with the initials "P.G.G.," which stood for Pinkerton Government Guard, the name the agency used during the Civil War.

The people of Missouri were furious about the bombing. The *Kansas City Times* wrote "there is no crime, however dastardly, which merits a retribution as savage and fiendish as the one which these men acting under the semblance of law have perpetrated." Every newspaper in the state condemned the attack on the Samuel farm. The revolver was proof that the Pinkertons, and railroad companies, were responsible for the attack.

The Pinkertons never captured the James Gang, even though they spent years trying.

A resolution was presented before the General Assembly on March 17, 1875, that offered amnesty for the James boys and the Youngers' actions during the war and a fair trial for crimes committed since 1865. The resolution called the desperadoes "too brave to be mean; and too gallant and honorable to betray a friend or break a promise." The resolution did not pass, although it won more than half the vote. (A two-thirds majority was required.)

Knowing that the gang had to be stopped, Missouri's Governor Thomas Crittenden, who was up for reelection, promised the voters to bring the gang to justice.

Early in 1882, Bob Ford (a member of the gang) told Crittenden that he knew Jesse James and wanted to help in his capture. He claimed he had met Jesse through gang member Dick Liddil, who was said to be secretly negotiating his own surrender terms.

Bob Ford met with Sheriff Timberlake of Clay County, and they came up with the following plan: Ford was to stay in Jesse's confidence and let the sheriff know the time and place of the gang's next job, even though they worried that Jesse might become suspicious when he heard the news that Bob's friend, Dick Liddil, had surrendered.

On April 3, 1882, Bob and his brother, Charlie Ford, were at Jesse's house. Jesse is claimed to have taken off his pistols, turned his back on the Fords, and stepped onto a chair in order to dust a picture that was hanging in the front room of the house. Bob Ford was then said to have pulled out a pearl-handled .44 and shot Jesse James in the back of the head.

Ford gave this written account of the shooting to Governor Crittenden:

> On the morning of April 3, Jess and I went downtown, as usual, before breakfast, for the papers. We got to the house about eight o'clock and sat down in the front room. Jess was sitting with his back to me, reading the *St. Louis Republican*. I picked up *The Times,* and the first thing I saw in big headlines was the story about Dick Liddil's surrender. Just then Mrs. James came

in and said breakfast was ready. Beside me was a chair with a shawl on it, and quick as a flash I lifted it and shoved the paper under. Jess couldn't have seen me, but he got up, walked over to the chair, picked up the shawl and threw it on the bed, and taking the paper, went out to the kitchen. I felt like the jig was up, but I followed and sat down at the table opposite Jess.

Mrs. James poured the coffee and then sat down at one end of the table. Jess spread the paper in front of him and began to look over the headlines. All at once Jess said: "Hello, here. The surrender of Dick Liddil" and he looked across at me with a glare in his eyes.

"Young man, I thought you told me you didn't know that Dick Liddil had surrendered," he said.

I told him I didn't know it.

"Well," he said, "it's very strange. He surrendered three weeks ago and you was right here in the neighborhood. It looks fishy."

He continued to glare at me, and I got up and went into the front room. In a minute I heard Jess push his chair back and walk to the door. He came in smiling, and said pleasantly: "Well Bob, it's all right anyway."

Instantly his real purpose flashed upon my mind. I knew I had not fooled him. He was too sharp for that. He knew at that moment as well as I did that I was there to betray him. But he was not going to kill me in the presence of his wife and children. He walked over to the bed, and deliberately unbuckled his belt, with four revolvers in it, and threw it on the bed. It was the first time in my life I had seen him without the belt on, and I knew he threw it off to further quiet any suspicions I might have.

He seemed to want to busy himself with something to make an impression on my mind that he had forgotten the incident at the breakfast table, and said: "That picture is awful dusty." There wasn't a speck of dust that I could see on the picture, but he stood a chair beneath it and then got upon it and began to dust the picture on the wall.

As he stood there, unarmed, with his back to me, it came to me suddenly, "Now or never is your chance. If you don't get him now he'll get you tonight." Without further thought or a moment's delay I pulled my revolver and leveled it as I sat. He heard the click as I cocked it with my thumb and started to turn as I pulled the trigger. The ball struck him just behind the ear and he fell like a log, dead. (Time-Life Books, *The Gunfighters*, p. 86)

Ford was tried before a jury in St. Joseph and sentenced to death, but two hours after the sentencing Governor Crittenden granted him a pardon.

To hear Bob Ford tell it, the man he claimed was Jesse James as much as committed suicide. But I believe the entire story was fabricated and was just a ploy to satisfy the public. Missouri would be rid of the gang and the governor would keep his reelection promises.

Rumors that it wasn't Jesse James who was shot started immediately and persist until this very day, and with very good reason. Ford's story just doesn't ring true.

It doesn't make sense that a man who didn't want to kill someone in his own home with his family present would knowingly allow his own life to be taken with his family present. (More evidence about the inaccuracy of Ford's story is included in Chapter 9.)

After doing intensive research on the James family, I can understand why Frank and Jesse, and the others, became outlaws. In their minds the war wasn't over.

When I visited the Jesse James Bank Museum in Liberty, Missouri, in March of 1996, the tour guide said she considered the James boys to be common thieves and murderers. She went on to say that other ex-Confederates went home and made a living on their own without resorting to crime. I remember thinking, *Well, why did they name the museum after Jesse James if they weren't proud of him?*

Many people feel that the James boys, the Younger brothers, and the other gang members were courageous for doing something about their situation instead of just sitting around allowing it to happen.

John Newman Edwards, who fought with Jesse and Frank in the Civil War, pinpointed the enigma of the James boys in his *Noted Guerrillas*:

> What else could Jesse James have done? In those evil days bad men in bands were doing bad things continually in the name of the law, order and vigilance committees. He had been a desperate guerrilla; he had fought under a black flag; he had made a name for terrible prowess along the border; he had survived

dreadful wounds; it was known that he would fight at any hour or in any way; he could not be frightened out from his native county; he could be neither intimidated nor robbed, and hence the wanton war waged upon Jesse and Frank James, and hence the reasons why to-day they are outlaws, and hence the reasons also that—outlaws as they are and proscribed in county, or state, or territory—they have more friends than the officers who hunt them, and more defenders than the armed men who seek to secure their bodies, dead or alive. . . .

By some intelligent people they are regarded as myths; by others as in league with the devil. They are neither, but they are uncommon men. Neither travels twice the same road. Neither tells the direction from which he came nor the direction in which he means to go. They are rarely together, but yet they are never far apart. There is a design in this—the calm, cool, deadly design of men who recognize the perils which beset them and who are not afraid to die. They traveled this way because if any so-called friend—tempted by the large rewards offered for the life of either —should seek to take it and succeed, the other, safe from the snare and free to do his worst, is pledged to avenge the brother slain through treachery, and avenge him surely. . . . the Jameses trust very few people—two probably out of every ten thousand. They come and go as silently as the leaves fall.

They never boast. They have many names and disguises. They speak low, are polite, deferential and accommadating. They do not kill save in stubborn self-defense. They have nothing in common with a murderer. They hate the highwayman and coward. They are outlaws, but they are not criminals, no matter what prejudiced public opinion may declare, or malignant partisan dislike make noisy with reiteration. The war made them desperate Guerrillas, and the harpies of the war—the robbers who came in the wake of it and the cut-throats who came to surface as the honorable combatants settled back again into civilized life —proscribed them and drove them into resistance. They were men who could not be bullied—who were too intrepid to be tyrannized over . . . . and who had surrendered in good faith, but who because of it did not intend any the less to have their rights and receive the treatment the balance of the Southern soldiers received. This is the summing up of the whole history of these two men since the Civil War. They were hunted, and they were human. They replied to proscription by defiance, ambushment by ambushment, musket shot by pistol shot, night attack by counterattack, charge by counter-charge, and so will they do, desperately and with splendid heroism, until the end.

I have always admired anyone who takes action against injustice. Some of the best memories of my father are when he took the family to the drive-in movie to see John Wayne westerns. We saw them all. Next to my father, John Wayne was my hero.

When my family and I watched *Tombstone,* a movie about Wyatt Earp, Doc Holliday, and the gunfight at the O.K. Corral, we wished we were related to men like that.

Little did we know that our wish was about to come true.

Chapter 4

★ ★ ★

A Whisper in My Ear

STANDING IN THE SMALL, peaceful Texas cemetery where many of my ancestors are buried, I feel as though I am being embraced by their love and approval.

I find myself staring at the granite tombstone of my great-grandfather, known as James Lafayette Courtney, wishing I could talk to him. The stories he could tell me would be treasured more than gold. The feelings of pride and admiration I have for this man among men are strong.

Blevins Cemetery sits on a hill with a majestic view of the rich farm land and rolling hills that stretch for miles toward the vast western horizon. The lay of the land reminds me of Kearney, Missouri, where my great-grandfather was born and reared. My ancestors are resting in a pretty place.

It's hard for me to comprehend that my great-grandfather (I refer to him as Grandpa, as everyone in the family called him that) was not only a legend in the Courtney family but a legend known around the world, because he was Jesse James—the most famous outlaw in American history.

I don't know why that fact is just now hitting me. I've heard the story all my life, and as a child I accepted what my parents told me just as I did the sun coming up every morning. But as I grew older, I started thinking maybe it was just one of those tall tales

> ★   ★   ★
>
> *There were six girls and one boy in my family.*
> *Daddy used to call us his little outlaws.*
>
> ★   ★   ★

Texans are famous for telling. After all, how could all of those books and movies be wrong? Every one of them agrees Bob Ford shot Jesse James dead on April 3, 1882.

After accepting the truth about Grandpa's real identity, evidence that could help prove my claim seemed to fall into my lap. It's been like finding buried treasure every day.

My first memory of hearing about Grandpa being Jesse James dates back to 1954, when I was around seven years old. Daddy's mother, Ida Courtney (more accurately James) Dorsett, died in January of that year, and Daddy wanted to go to Blevins Cemetery to visit her gravesite. Blevins is a small farming community about thirty miles south of Waco.

My parents loaded five of their seven children into the family car and off we went. I remember feeling so crowded. I couldn't wait until we got there; it seemed so far away from Austin. Daddy started telling us stories about "Ma" (his mother) and her father, Grandpa Courtney, probably to quiet us down.

He said that Grandpa rode with the Youngers, and that if anyone rode up to his house at night he would blow out all the coal-oil lamps and lay down across the doorway, with his pistol cocked, so that if anyone entered the house they would trip over him. I remember Daddy saying that Grandpa Courtney was Jesse James.

He really got our attention when he told us about Grandpa's buried treasure. I remember when we returned home, I got a spoon out of the kitchen drawer and started digging in the yard for gold. After awhile I needed a drink of water and went into the house. While I was in the house, Mama slipped outside and put some coins into the hole I had been digging. When I went back outside and dug a little deeper, I thought I'd struck it rich! I didn't

★ ★ ★

My great-grandfather's son Byron said
there were tens of thousands of dollars
of gold buried by Grandpa in different
locations. Grandpa left maps with
coded messages telling of their location.

★ ★ ★

realize that most children weren't raised on stories of buried treasure in their grandparents' yard!

When I was a child I didn't know who Jesse James was, and when I became a teenager I was ashamed to tell anyone about it. A relative had been in trouble with the law and people seemed to condemn the entire family for it. As I grew older I realized the trouble my relative had was small compared to the skeletons hiding in the closets of the very people who had condemned my family.

As a teenager I thought I knew everything. I remember thinking my parents were so naive for believing that Grandpa was actually Jesse James. After all, didn't they know he had been killed many years before any of us were even born? Didn't they know their history? At the most, I thought, Grandpa had probably just ridden with Frank and Jesse.

Well, I've always heard what goes around comes around. Now when I tell someone about Grandpa being Jesse James I see that doubting look come into their eyes. However, "that look" disappears quickly when they see my evidence.

All of my research started in 1995, when I was sitting at the kitchen table reading Grandpa's diary. In a flash of realization or inspiration—whatever it was, my feeling cannot be logically explained—I suddenly knew that Grandpa was Jesse James. I had read nothing that said, "I was Jesse James"; it was as though he whispered his secret in my ear.

I kept it to myself a couple of days, just thinking about it, and then I decided to tell my husband and daughter. Joe and Teresa were in the living room watching television when I walked in and said, "I know y'all are going to think I'm crazy, but Grandpa Courtney really was Jesse James."

They just looked at me. I could read their minds; they were thinking, *Well, she's lost her mind.* When they finally spoke, almost in unison, they said, "How do you get that?"

I know it sounded feeble, but I said, "I don't know how I know . . . I just know that he was." At that point I didn't have any proof.

Believe me, I've had many battles to fight since I accepted Grandpa's true identity.

The first skirmish occurred when I tried convincing members of my immediate family that Grandpa was Jesse James. I could understand that they thought I was crazy in the beginning; after all, I had believed the historically accepted story about Jesse James for most of my forty-seven years.

My daughter Teresa accepted the story after one night of thinking it over. She woke up the next morning and said, "Well, I always heard he rode with the gang, so he could be Jesse James." My husband and sons took much longer. It has to be understood that at this point I had no evidence to back up my claim. All I had was Grandpa's diary—and pure instinct.

I'll never forget that August day in 1995 when Joe realized that Grandpa really was Jesse James. We live in the country and had given up trying to have a mailbox after one was stolen and the other was shot to pieces. I guess some folks can get pretty bored. Anyway, we have a post office box in town and drive there to get our mail every day. We had received a letter from one of my cousins out of state, and I opened it and started reading it aloud while we were driving back home. The cousin had enclosed a letter from my father's deceased sister, Irene, dated February 22, 1973. She was answering questions about Grandpa Courtney that the cousin had apparently asked her in an earlier letter.

While reading Aunt Irene's letter I came to this part: "Mama also said something about Grandpa knowing something about Jesse James—when I see you I will tell you more about that—as it might have been a family secret." The funny thing is, I had not mentioned anything about knowing the true identity of Grandpa to my cousin. That's all it took for Joe. He got chills all over and has believed my story from that day on.

My sons took a lot more convincing. My oldest son, Danny, became fully convinced after seeing family photographs that matched James family photographs. He even started calling him Grandpa James. My other son, Johnny, wouldn't commit one way or the other for a long time. Clint Whitehead, a family friend, told me later on that when he and Johnny were hunting dove at our tank dam, Johnny looked at him and said, "That's pretty cool isn't it?" He was referring to the story about Grandpa. The next time Johnny and I talked, he said, "You know I believe you, don't you?" Victory at last!

I don't believe Meredith, my daughter-in-law, knew what to think. With all of the names and name changes to remember, I guess it was pretty confusing. But the excitement around our house was contagious, and after awhile she caught the fever.

My mother didn't need any convincing because she had known it for years. She just didn't have any proof.

I have had many spirited conversations with people who view Jesse James as a common thief and murderer. They couldn't be more mistaken. Generally, people from the South view him as a Confederate hero while some people from the northern section of this country see nothing admirable about him at all. I have found that most people, from all parts of the country, view him as a folk hero.

Trying to decide whether to reveal the truth about Jesse James to the world has not been easy. Many people before me have made similar claims and were eventually proven wrong. Knowing that I, and my family, would be subjected to a lot of criticism didn't make the decision any easier. Then I realized that Jesse James was a man who fought hard for what he believed in. The truth was made known to me for a reason, and I believe it has to be told for Grandpa's sake and for the sake of history.

It wasn't only my parents who had tried to tell me the truth about Grandpa, but other family members as well.

In the winter of 1985, I had gone to see Aunt Judy, the wife of Daddy's brother, Bud. I really enjoyed talking to her and knew I could satisfy my sweet tooth at her house because she always had plenty of delicious homemade cookies around. Mama spoiled us when we were growing up by always having mouth-watering homemade desserts after supper every night. Having a sweet tooth seems to run in the family.

Aunt Judy and I were sitting at her kitchen table, talking and laughing, when she said, "Did you know your grandmother's maiden name was James, not Courtney?"

I remember thinking that at least Daddy wasn't the *only* person telling such a tale. She went on to say that Grandpa Courtney had told his daughter Ida (my grandmother) the truth about his real identity because she was his favorite child and more like him than the rest of his children.

My only response was to say, "Aunt Judy, that can't be true. Jesse James was killed a long time ago." She looked at me with those knowing old eyes and said, "Betty Gail, it is true. You can't believe everything you read! You need to know who your family really is." She got up from her chair and went to her bedroom closet. When she came back to the table she handed me an envelope with my name written on it. I opened it and found one of Grandpa's treasure maps inside telling how to find $30,000 in gold. Aunt Judy said she wanted me to have it.

At this point, I was still believing the story that was told in history books and movies—not the family stories. But at the same time I knew that those in my family weren't the type of people to make something like this up. They were sincere.

I started remembering the stories about the James Gang that Daddy told me as I was growing up. He was trying to feed and clothe seven kids and didn't have the time to waste making up tales. I thought it was possible that Grandpa rode with the James Gang, but I couldn't believe he *was* Jesse James.

I really regret not asking Daddy and Uncle Bud more about our ancestors before they died. Daddy died June 5, 1966. As Mama put it, "Your daddy was 'much a man.'" In my estimation he could do no wrong.

Mama said he was his mother's favorite child and that his brothers and sisters called him "Ma's man." He loved his family and was very tender toward his children. I couldn't have asked for better parents. I had a very happy childhood.

My brother, Jesse Wayne, remembers times when the sheriff's department couldn't arrest someone they had a warrant for so they would come to our house and deputize Daddy. He, too, had the reputation of being fearless. There aren't many men like Daddy and his brothers anymore. They were a special breed.

Uncle Bud died suddenly from a heart attack in 1981 and Aunt Judy died in 1992. Uncle Boy (Daddy's younger brother), who compared in size to a pro-football lineman, died in 1987. My sources for family history were quickly disappearing.

With two kids in high school and the oldest about to enter college, I was very busy, and I tried pushing all thoughts of digging into my family's history to the back of my mind. It didn't work. I kept getting a strong feeling that I had to find something, but I didn't know what I was looking for or how to find it. There was a definite feeling in the air, like something big was about to happen. I felt driven. It was an undeniable force.

I started calling relatives, trying to get as much information about my family as possible.

One of my cousins, Tim Dorsett, was said to have a lot of information about our Dorsett ancestors. (Grandpa's daughter Ida had married Bill Dorsett.) When I contacted him, he told me that my father still had a sister living and her name was Opal. I hadn't been around many members of Daddy's family since I was very young, so I didn't have any recollection of her. When I called her I was hoping she would remember me, and to my pleasure she did. Arrangements were made for me to visit her at home.

After arriving, I discovered that she was ill and very frail, dying of cancer. She reminded me so much of Daddy. She was very gentle and caring, and seemed to have a great inner strength. She never complained. We talked of Daddy and the rest of the family.

"Aunt Opal, I heard that Grandpa Courtney rode with the James Gang. Did you ever hear anything about that?"

She was sitting on the couch and looked right at me. With a *humph* she said, "I heard he *was* Jesse James."

I just shook my head and said, "Boy, you can hear just about anything, can't you?"

Aunt Opal just looked at me and shook her head. I guess she felt too bad to put up with my stupidity.

I could see that she was serious, so I asked her if there was any proof. She said that she didn't know of any, but that her family was not in the habit of lying. I told her I didn't mean to imply that they were, but that no one would ever believe such a thing without proof. She told me about cousins that I had never heard of until that moment. They were elderly second cousins who had lived with Grandpa a big part of their childhood. After getting their names and telephone numbers, I left, knowing she didn't feel well.

I regretted not knowing Aunt Opal until it was almost too late, and I kept in close contact with her until she died. We really enjoyed getting to know each other. She told me so many things about my family that I would never have known if we hadn't met. I just wanted to grab hold of her and not let go.

My next goal was to contact my long-lost cousins. I wanted to find out everything I could about a side of my family that I had never known. I also wanted to find out more about Grandpa Courtney.

I called the eldest cousin first and explained that I was doing genealogical research on the paternal side of my family. Being a genealogist herself, she said she would be happy to share what information she had with me. But I made a bad mistake when I asked her about Grandpa being Jesse James on the telephone. It immediately put her on guard.

She did provide me much information on my ancestors. I discovered there were Native Americans on my father's side of the family. I knew there was on my maternal side.

It turns out that Grandpa Courtney's wife, Mary Ellen, was part Choctaw. I obtained a copy of an affidavit that had to be filed with the government before Mary Ellen could get her C.D.I.B. (Certificate of Degree of Indian Blood). To be a recognized member of one of the Five Civilized Tribes you have to prove you are a direct descendant of a registered member of one of the tribes. I have searched for her C.D.I.B but have not yet located it.

My cousin invited my family and me to her home, which was a four-hour trip from where we live in the Texas Hill Country. She had old photographs of Grandpa and his family that she wanted us to see.

On the way there, I told my family that if we found a photograph of my great-great-grandmother showing that she was missing an arm, I would know that I was 100% right about Grandpa being Jesse James. My research on Jesse James had informed me of his mother's arm amputation after the Pinkerton bombing.

When we arrived, the cousin gave my daughter Teresa an old family photo album to look through. Suddenly, she became very excited. There was a photo of my great-great-grandmother—and she was clearly missing an arm!

The fact that Zerelda James Samuel (Jesse James' mother) was missing the same arm made it certain in my mind that the two women were the same person. They certainly looked alike, but the only photograph I had of her up until that time was from the shoulders up. The missing arm made the match undeniable.

We contained our excitement because of the cool response I had received from our cousin when I mentioned Jesse James earlier. I think she felt as if she had to protect us from a shameful family secret.

Her husband told us a story about a couple of plumbers who came to their home and noticed a big photograph of Grandpa and his brother hanging on the wall. With a mischievous twinkle in his eye, he told us that the plumbers said, "They sure look like a couple of desperadoes."

If they only knew. . . .

I remember a telephone conversation with the elderly cousin's sister when she asked me out of the clear blue if I knew that Grandpa had known Jesse James personally. I almost fell through the floor. I had been hesitant to ask her if she knew anything about Grandpa being Jesse James after my experience with her sister. When I asked her what Grandpa had said about Jesse, she "beat around the bush" awhile and then said that she hadn't asked him any questions about how he knew him.

I guess Grandpa did know Jesse James personally. They were one and the same person.

During one visit with the oldest cousin she mentioned that she had always heard that Grandpa was really someone else and that those were terrible times on the Missouri border in those days. I told her I wanted to hear the truth no matter what, but no amount of coaxing would make her reveal any more information.

Chapter 5

★　　★　　★

On the Trail of Discovery

O N OUR WAY TO find out more in Missouri, I could picture desperadoes, their long dusters flowing in the wind, riding over the gently rolling hills of Kearney, Missouri. I could hear their horses' hoofs pounding the earth, carrying the riders swiftly along. I wished I could go back in time and ride with them, just to see them in action.

It's hard to believe the destruction that occurred throughout this beautiful land in the War Between the States. Those ancient hills with ponds of life-giving water nestled in their valleys could tell us many tales if only they could speak.

The people of Kearney were easygoing and friendly, reminding me of the way people were in my hometown of Austin, when it was a much smaller city.

We could hardly wait to arrive at the James Farm. We drove straight through from Texas, and as we pulled into town just before dark a light snow started to fall. That really excited us; Central Texas doesn't get much snow. There was no way we were going to wait until the next morning to see the farm after driving so many miles to get there. It was an approximate five-minute drive from downtown Kearney, so we could just make it before it was too dark to see. I will never forget the first glimpse of the entrance gate and the sign that read: "The Home of Frank and Jesse James." It seemed impossible that the farm where my great-grandfather was born is now a tourist attraction and museum.

The next morning we were up bright and early, raring to go to the farm. Driving through the entrance gate and up the driveway, we could see the farmhouse off to the northwest. The house is on a hill with a creek winding around it. The snow on the ground and in the branches of the trees added to the magic I was feeling.

As we walked up the pathway to the farmhouse, I felt as though I was exactly where I should be. We stepped onto the porch and walked in the front door. I felt like I was home. I was trying to listen to the tour guide and control my emotions at the same time. I felt my ancestors around me, and I knew deep within my heart that everything I had been told was true, that my great-grandfather was Jesse James. I couldn't even guess at how I and all of my relatives came about, living in Texas. I knew if he died in Missouri in 1882, all of us were at least an impossibility. There had to be more to the story.

But now, as we stepped where the James family stepped and looked at what they had looked at, I felt connected. I felt like shouting the truth to everyone there.

The next morning we reluctantly left Kearney to go to St. Joseph to tour the house where Jesse James was supposedly shot. One of the main attractions was the bullet hole high on the wall where Jesse was said to have stood on a chair to straighten a picture and was shot in the back of the head. The bullet purportedly went right through his head, entering the wall and leaving behind the legendary bullet hole.

The entire time we were in St. Joseph I rushed the rest of my family because I wanted to get back to Kearney and the farm.

We arrived back at the James Farm later that day and decided to tour the museum, which is separate from the farm but located on the same grounds. While touring the museum we saw a large portrait of Zerelda James Samuel displayed on the wall, and we decided to compare a photograph of my great-great-grandmother to it. I was holding our wallet-size photo up to the portrait when Mr. Breckenridge, an employee of the James Farm, walked up and asked what we were doing. I told him we were comparing the women and commented about how they looked identical.

He asked if we were associated with Waggoner Carr and his

group. (At that point in time I didn't even know a Waggoner Carr, or that he was involved in the Jesse James controversy. Carr is an ex-attorney general of Texas.) After I told him that we weren't, he said that the only reason the women looked alike is because they were both old and didn't have any teeth. In a voice loud with anger he said that all of the Texans who come up there claiming that Jesse lived and died in Texas didn't know what they were talking about. He said Jesse was born in Missouri and died in Missouri.

I was insulted because I had made no claims to him of any kind. I thought I answered him in a normal tone, but my family informed otherwise. "I don't care what you think," I said. "No one is trying to take anything away from Missouri. He was born here, but he did not die here." I was basing that statement on nothing but my gut feelings, but I knew I was right.

Breckenridge told us that we were in luck because George Warfel, a portrait artist and illustrator asked by the James family to assist in authenticating photographs, just happened to be in the museum. Warfel resides in Florida. Then Breckenridge informed us that the museum had documents to prove where Zerelda Samuel was until she died. I told Breckenridge that they may have known where Zerelda was every minute, but they sure didn't know where Jesse had been.

We had created quite a disturbance by that time. Everyone in the museum was staring and trying to hear what was going on. Warfel, who had been downstairs in a meeting, came into the room. Breckenridge asked him to take a look at our picture and Warfel agreed, looking like he was thinking, *Oh no, not another group claiming to be related to Jesse James.* We introduced ourselves and he casually took my picture. When he looked at it, he stopped dead in his tracks and asked where I got the photograph.

I told him it was a family picture, and that I would like to compare it to a different photograph of Zerelda in the museum that we had seen. He said he knew just the one I was talking about. We walked to the portrait and I held my photograph up to it with trembling hands. He looked from me to the portrait on the wall several times, and then he began taking measurements with his hands of my great-great-grandmother's face. He measured different parts of her face, the ear to the chin, the nose, the distance between the nose and lip, and the forehead. With every measurement he took he confirmed that they matched. He then said the match was real close and asked me to send a copy of my photo to his home in Florida for further testing.

I tried to conceal the fact that I was overcome with emotion.

While waiting for Warfel's assessment of our photo, I decided to try to find an expert for a second opinion on whether my great-great-grandmother was indeed Jesse James' mother.

My family and I could tell just by looking that the family photographs we had acquired from my father and other family members matched photographs of the James/Samuel family. But we're not experts, and we knew we needed an expert's opinion of the photographs to lend credence to our claim. Warfel had recommended that the photographs be compared with a computer, using a method he called "computer graphics analysis."

Computer graphics companies that I contacted had no idea what I was talking about. It was suggested that I contact the Texas Department of Public Safety (DPS) and talk to their experts.

I followed their advice and was given the name of a forensic artist in Corpus Christi, Texas. I called her and she agreed to examine the photos. She cautioned me that she would give her honest opinion, and it might not be what I wanted to hear. When I called for the results she said it looked like the same woman to her and then suggested that I see an internationally noted forensic artist in the Austin office of the Texas DPS that she felt could give a more accurate opinion of the photographs.

When Teresa and I arrived at the DPS in Austin, I showed the forensic artist the family photographs that I had collected along with known photographs of the James and Samuel family. I told her that I thought the man in the photograph that was said to be Jesse James was an impostor. It was the most famous photograph of him. She put the known photo of Jesse James and the photo of my great-grandfather on her computer screen, which was then projected onto a large screen on the wall. Details that were not noticeable before became apparent because of the enlargement.

I was rummaging through my folder trying to find another photo when she asked me why I thought the man in the famous photo was an impostor. I looked up to see her pointing at the

historically accepted photo of Jesse James. I told her that he had to
be an impostor if my great-grandfather was Jesse James because
the man in the picture, believed to be Jesse James, was killed by
Bob Ford in 1882 and buried in Mt. Olivet Cemetery in Kearney,
Missouri. (This meeting occurred in the summer of 1995. An exhumation of that grave in Missouri was taking place that same
summer.)

She then asked what I thought about the two photos displayed
on the screen. She was indicating a crease that was perpendicular
to Grandpa's jawline, and then pointing to an identical crease in
the same location on the known picture of Jesse James. She said
that the crease was odd in the fact that it looked like the jawbone
didn't quite meet, almost as if it had been broken. All of the lines
and marks along the crease were identical in both photographs.

I just stood there, staring and speechless. Again she asked
what I thought. By the time I could finally speak I said, "I'd say
you were a damned liar if I wasn't seeing this with my own eyes!"

She laughed and pointed out that the slant of the eyes was the
same in both men, and the tilt of their noses (which was a little
unusual) was the same.

"How can this be?" I could hardly think straight. The forensic artist just shrugged her shoulders and shook her head.

I knew for a fact that Grandpa didn't die until 1943—so who
was buried in the grave that was supposed to hold the remains of
Jesse James? It certainly wasn't Jesse James.

The forensic artist was impressed with my photographs. Not
only were my family photos of Grandpa consistent with the famous
photo of Jesse, but other family photographs were consistent with
known photos of Zerelda (Jesse's mother), Archie Samuel (Jesse's
half-brother), Dr. Reuben Samuel (Jesse's stepfather), Zee
Mimms (Jesse's first cousin), and Jesse Edwards James (Zee
Mimms' son).

While examining the photographs of Grandpa, the forensic
artist noted that Grandpa was a spiffy dresser. Family legend has
it that he even wore a string tie while plowing his fields. Jesse
James was also known for being a well-dressed man, and for liking
to have his picture taken.

Grandpa had numerous pictures taken of himself and his
family. I know now, from doing genealogical research on other

family lines, that having several photographs is rare. I even felt fortunate to find one early photograph of my other great-grandparents because it was expensive to have them made in the 1800s.

My daughter had noticed that the gown worn by my great-great-grandmother in a photograph was identical to a gown Zerelda James Samuel was pictured wearing in a book (Phillip Steele's *Jesse and Frank James: The Family History,* p. 25). The forensic artist made arrangements for a DPS photography supervisor to scan the two photographs through a special computer to determine if the dresses matched. This computer is capable of lifting a handprint off an article of clothing. The computer proved what I already knew—the dresses were identical. The photography supervisor commented that there couldn't have been very many little old ladies running around Missouri that looked just alike, wearing the same dress and missing an arm.

My family photographs speak for themselves.

The forensic artist believed that in order for me to prove that my great-grandfather was Jesse James it would probably have to come down to Mitochondrial DNA testing as it is an exact science. Even though she was impressed, she would not state unequivocally that the photos were 100% proof because forensic art is not an exact science.

Since the meeting with the forensic artist, Visionics Corporation, world leaders in face recognition technology, have concluded through computerized matching that my family photos match the known photos of the James/Samuel family. Visionics Corporation's Faceit PC is an "award winning software engine that uses sophisticated algorithms for pattern recognition developed by Visionics' renowned research team. These algorithms are an outgrowth of recent discoveries on how the human brain recognizes faces and have been shown to outperform all other leading facial recognition algorithms in recent U.S. Government testing. The same technology that goes into Faceit PC is used for security applications in international airports, border crossings, and a multitude of other access control applications." (www.Faceit.com)

I am willing to compare my Mitochondrial DNA with Zerelda's MtDNA, or my great-grandfather's MtDNA, but not the MtDNA of the man in the questioned grave that is claimed to be

Jesse James. What I would learn about the MtDNA exhumed from that grave would prove the futility of that.

George Warfel's evaluation of the photograph I had mailed to him for further testing was different from the opinion of the forensic artist at the Texas Department of Public Safety. But in the reply I received from him he stated that he thought I should rely on the opinion of the Texas DPS because their method of measurement is more accurate. He then added that, in his opinion, the photos of Zerelda and my great-great-grandmother didn't match.

I called Warfel and told him I didn't quite understand what he was telling me, because he was talking out of both sides of his mouth. On one hand he told me to consider the conclusions of the DPS to be correct, but on the other hand he was saying the pictures didn't match. He just laughed. During this telephone conversation he did admit he was flabbergasted by the photograph.

Warfel is a very nice gentleman, and I appreciated his help, but I decided his opinion could be biased due to his long association and friendship with the Missouri group.

It was time to find out more about Mitochondrial DNA.

Chapter 6

★   ★   ★

Exhumations of the Questioned Grave

CCORDING TO THE *KEARNEY COURIER'S* "Special Collectors' Edition," Zerelda James Samuel had the remains that were buried in 1882 under the name Jesse Woodson James exhumed from the yard of the family farm on July 29, 1902, so that they could be interred in Mt. Olivet Cemetery, which is located approximately three miles from the farm. It's my opinion that Zerelda probably wanted the body buried in the farmyard in the first place so she could make sure no one could dig it up and discover their secret—that Jesse was not the person buried there. She probably thought that since twenty years had passed it would be safe to rebury the remains in Mt. Olivet Cemetery.

Tim Howard, aka Jesse Edwards James (purported to be Jesse's son), was present at the disinterment. He examined the skull and noticed a bullet hole behind the ear but found no evidence of an exit hole.

In 1978 more remains that were claimed to belong to Jesse James were exhumed from the original gravesite at the James Farm. Initial reports in 1882 said the bullet from Bob Ford's pistol which shot the man they claimed was Jesse James was a .44-caliber, but a .38-caliber bullet was discovered in the coffin. A human tooth, a toe bone, an atlas vertebra, and a bone that couldn't be identified were put in a Tupperware container and reburied in the

★   ★   ★

*When my family and I toured the
James Farm in March of 1996, the tour
guide told how Zerelda James Samuel sold
pebbles for a quarter a piece from the
grave that was claimed to hold the
remains of her beloved son, Jesse James.
The guide went on to say that when
Zerelda would run out of pebbles to sell
off the grave, she would replenish her sup-
ply by taking a bucket to the creek near
her home and filling it up with pebbles
from the creek bed to place on the reported
grave of Jesse James.*

*This story reinforces my theory that
her son, Jesse James, was not the man in
the grave. From a mother's viewpoint, if
one of my beloved children died, I cannot
imagine selling pebbles off of the grave for
profit, or for any other reason.*

★   ★   ★

original gravesite at the farm. This 1978 exhumation was not done by scientists; it was done by Clay County Park officials.

It is evident that with two unscientific exhumations done prior to the 1995 exhumation the remains have been tampered with numerous times. I believe this tampering affected the DNA results of the 1995 exhumation.

The 1995 exhumation of the questioned grave was begun on July 17. This exhumation was done to "silence those claiming some relation to the famous outlaw," according to the Ross/Barr group (who claim relation to Jesse James). The exhumation was led by Professor of Law and Forensic Sciences James E. Starrs, of George Washington University in Washington, D.C. After comparing Mitochondrial DNA donated by Robert Jackson and Mark

Nikkel, descendants of Susan James (Jesse's sister), to Mitochondrial DNA from a tooth (the origin of which is very questionable), Starrs concluded that the man in the grave was Jesse James.

Mitochondrial DNA is passed down through the maternal line. For instance, Zerelda James Samuel would have passed her Mitochondrial DNA (MtDNA) on to all of her children, including her sons, but only her daughter could pass it on to the next generation.

According to the A&E documentary "In Search of Jesse James," no MtDNA was obtained from the bones exhumed in Mt. Olivet Cemetery by Starrs' exhumation team in July of 1995. They were too deteriorated from water. No Mitochondrial DNA could be extracted from the fifteen teeth in the scientists' first efforts. Shortly after the July exhumation Judge Vic Howard ordered the tooth encased in the Tupperware container in 1978 at the James Farm to be exhumed because Starrs thought he may need it for extracting Mitochondrial DNA for testing. Starrs was quoted in the *Kearney Courier* as saying, "That tooth could be the tooth that tells the tale." When the container was unearthed, it was discovered that the tooth that was supposed to be there was missing. According to the *Kearney Courier*'s February 29, 1996, issue, "only one tooth and one head hair retrieved from the James Farm Museum carried sufficient MtDNA for testing." *The tooth used for MtDNA testing did not come from the questioned grave in Mt. Olivet Cemetery.*

When Clay County took ownership of the James Farm in 1976, five teeth were found on the property: two human teeth (the sex of the person, or persons, they came from is unknown), two dog teeth, and one hog tooth. The two human teeth may have very well belonged to a member of the James family, but which one is not known.

On the A&E documentary, Starrs said, "I'll go out on the deep end . . . and say I feel with a reasonable degree of scientific certainty that we have the remains of Jesse James. Everything that we have indicates a direct relationship to Jesse James. . . . And that's as far as we can go and as far as I am willing to go. There is nothing to exclude and everything to include."

Starrs announced his findings at the Opryland Hotel in

Nashville, Tennessee, and at the reception held afterward he sold autographed T-shirts.

The following findings from Starrs' exhumation team were reported along with Starrs' conclusions. Quoted material is from the *Kearney Courier,* February 29, 1996:

- "MtDNA tests were done on several bones and teeth but only one tooth and head hair retrieved from the James Farm Museum carried sufficient MtDNA for testing. Test results from the hair still are being formulated."

I believe the above statement confirms my belief about the questionable origin of the tooth that was used for MtDNA comparison testing to the MtDNA of Susan James' living descendants. It was announced that "only one tooth and head hair retrieved from the James Farm Museum carried sufficient MtDNA for testing." I don't believe there is any scientific evidence documenting who this tooth belonged to or exactly where it was actually found. Since the tooth was retrieved from the James Farm it may have been, and in all probability was, one of the two human teeth found in 1976 by Clay County Park officials, indicating that the teeth probably did belong to a James family member since the Jameses had lived there since the 1840s. This finding suggests that Starrs' conclusions of Jesse James being the person in the questioned grave in Mt. Olivet Cemetery are not based on documented scientific evidence since the MtDNA scientists used for testing came from a questionable origin.

The same lack of evidence applies to the hair retrieved from the James Farm. Whose hair was it? I don't believe the origin of the hair can be positively verified. I have tried to obtain the results of the MtDNA tests on the hair in question but no one I've contacted at the James Farm or the *Kearney Courier* knows the answer to that.

- "Toxicology—Bones and hair were tested for morphine, codeine, and cocaine. None were found. The lack of evidence was the only part of the scientific evidence revealing no evidence."

- "The 'legendary bullet hole' in the wall—The hole was purportedly created when Jesse's fatal bullet exited his skull and ripped open a wall in his home in St. Joseph. Last Thursday

Starrs said he was certain the bullet never exited the head. During the presentation, however, he softened his stance.

"Without being able to fully reconstruct the skull, he said, scientists were unable to ascertain whether it exited, although he thought it did."

It's my opinion that Starrs could have been "crawfishing" on the finding concerning whether the bullet exited the skull or not because the bullet hole in the wall of the house in St. Joseph is one of the main attractions for tourists. First Starrs said the bullet didn't exit the skull; then he claimed he "thought" it did. Could Starrs have "softened his stance" on other findings?

John Cayton from the Kansas City Crime Lab stated on the A&E documentary "In Search of Jesse James" that he doesn't believe the bullet exited the skull. Starrs said in the same documentary they found a clear entrance wound but no exit wound.

- "Handwriting—Document specialist Duayne Dillon said handwriting from J. Frank Dalton and Jesse James were clearly different."

J. Frank Dalton claimed to be Jesse James in 1947. It seems to me that whether or not Dalton's handwriting matched the handwriting claimed to be that of Jesse James is irrelevant. In my opinion, Dillon still didn't prove that the handwriting claimed to be that of Jesse James was in fact his.

- "Second exhumation—Dr. Michael Finnegan of Kansas State University said remains exhumed in 1978 from the original grave of Jesse James revealed a 34 to 42 year old Caucasian who died from 100 to 150 years ago and had dental problems.

  "In the 1995 exhumation at Mount Olivet Cemetery, Finnegan said the remains belonged to someone who was a 23 to 68 year old male Caucasian from 5 feet 8 inches to 5 feet 10 inches in height, and who was buried face down, indicating a reburial.

  "A circumferential saw mark on the skull was indicative of autopsies performed during the 1880s. Time of death was before 1902. 'They are entirely consistent with what is historically known about Jesse James,' Finnegan said."

If you think about it, they could be describing any number of people. The finding of the saw mark on the skull did prove that the remains belonged to the same man placed in the original grave in 1882, but it did not prove that man was Jesse James.

Reports on the findings continue below:

• "The bullet found in the July exhumation is not believed to be the one that killed him. Scientists and historians believe Jesse took the bullet when he was trying to surrender near Lexington. Accounts said he was wounded in the right lung and scientists said the bullet was recovered in the chest area.

"Historian Ted Yeatman said Jesse went to Nashville soon after the shooting to recover. A doctor there could not remove the bullet.

"Firearms Specialist John Cayton of the Kansas City Regional Criminalists Laboratory said the bullet had been shot from a 1851 Colt Navy Revolver, a common sidearm during and after the Civil War.

"A 38-caliber bullet had been found in the original grave. [Another .38-caliber bullet was found during the 1995 exhumation. Where was the .45-caliber bullet that was claimed to be the fatal bullet?] The fatal bullet, according to historical accounts, was shot from either a .44 caliber Smith & Wesson or a .45 caliber silver-mounted and pearl-handled Colt Revolver."

• "Teeth—Gold fillings in teeth discovered in the grave were consistent with what is known about Jesse James. It is documented, too, that when Jesse James, Jr., dug up his father in 1902 to move him to Mount Olivet, he recognized the skull by the bullet wound and the gold fillings."

Jesse Edwards James (referred to above as Jesse James, Jr.) probably did recognize the skull of his father by the bullet wound and he probably did recognize his father by the gold fillings in the teeth. But just because he recognized these features doesn't mean his father was Jesse James. It's important to remember the following:

1. Jesse Edwards James was given the name Tim Howard at

birth and only took the name of Jesse Edwards James after his father died.

2. Findings reported on the teeth exhumed from the 1995 exhumation showed that they were corroded and heavily stained from tobacco use. The person the teeth belonged to clearly had dental problems.

    Jesse's first cousin and fellow gang member, Wood Hite, had decayed, stained teeth indicating he had dental problems.

    Since history reports that Jesse didn't use tobacco, it sounds as if the scientists could be describing Wood Hite's teeth.

3. The man killed on April 3, 1882, was known as Thomas Howard (supposedly an alias for Jesse James) and he also signed letters using that name.

4. A gun owned by Thomas Howard had the initials "W.H." and "T.H." Common sense tells me those initials stood for Wood Hite and Thomas Howard. I believe it was Wood Hite who used the alias of Thomas Howard, not Jesse James.

In the A&E documentary "In Search of Jesse James," Starrs stated that Missouri law prohibited him from exhuming Jesse's mother, Zerelda, for Mitochondrial DNA testing because she died of natural causes. I decided to check the Missouri law concerning exhumations myself, since I had found other discrepancies about the exhumation that have been reported as fact. After checking Vernon's Annotated Missouri Statutes, section 214.205, I discovered that there is no law that prevents Zerelda from being exhumed. It seems to me that Starrs, a law professor, should have been aware of that.

Was someone afraid of the possibility that had Zerelda been exhumed her MtDNA wouldn't have matched the MtDNA of the remains from the questioned grave, proving once and for all whether the man buried in that grave was her son or not?

Anne Dingus of *Texas Monthly* magazine stated that "other factors cast doubt on the scientist's conclusions concerning the 1995 exhumation of the grave in question. For example, contrary

★ ★ ★

Scientists reported that the man in the questioned grave, assumed by them to be Jesse James, was a regular tobacco user. Yet Zee Mimms testified under oath that the man she was married to was Jesse James and that he did not use tobacco. History backs up her story—Jesse James did not use tobacco.

Why Zee Mimms went along with the plan to identify her husband's body as the body of Jesse James is not known. It could be that since her husband was dead anyway it would be a chance to help her first cousin, Jesse James, start a new life.

★ ★ ★

to reported history, the body was buried face down, and the disintegrated casket was made of wood, not metal."

Starrs appeared baffled when a metal coffin was not found. The James Farm has the metal coffin on display that they claim Jesse was buried in.

Zee Mimms testified at the coroner's inquest held after the purported shooting of Jesse James that "Jesse never drank, smoked nor chewed" (The *Daily Gazette,* St. Joseph, Missouri, April 5, 1882). Again, the teeth removed from the exhumation site and examined by Dr. Mark Stoneking of Penn State University were reported to be corroded and heavily stained, showing the man buried in the questioned grave was a regular tobacco chewer. This finding differed from historical accounts that Jesse James did not use tobacco.

My great-grandfather did not use tobacco.

History reports that Jesse James was missing the tip of his middle left finger, but the exhumation did not address this issue. Zee Mimms (Jesse's first cousin and purportedly his wife) seemed confused on that issue herself. When she was asked at the inquest how old her husband was, she wasn't sure. And when asked if he was disfigured in any way, her response was "no sir, I believe not." Then when it was explained they were referring to any wounds on his hand, she said that he had the end of his finger shot off but couldn't remember which one, possibly a middle finger. Most women know the age of their husbands and would certainly know if they were missing fingers. I believe Zee may have been married to the man who was killed, but not married to Jesse James.

George Warfel said that a photograph of Jesse James and Archie Clements was found recently that appeared to have been taken toward the end of the Civil War. His left hand and fingers were clearly visible, and there was no missing finger. This is important because both Phillip Steele and George Warfel have claimed that Jesse's finger was shot off before leaving the farm. Jesse was around thirteen or fourteen when he left the family farm, so by the time the photograph with Archie was taken, Jesse would have already lost the tip of his middle left finger.

Was Jesse James missing the tip of his middle left finger, or was the man Bob Ford shot missing the tip of his middle left finger?

The remains in the questioned grave in Mt. Olivet Cemetery need not be disturbed again. The only grave that needs to be exhumed in that cemetery holds the remains of Zerelda James Samuel. Then, if my great-grandfather's remains are exhumed, his MtDNA can be compared to Zerelda's MtDNA in order to find out if he was her son.

I can only hope that Zerelda's remains have not been disturbed.

In my opinion the 1995 exhumation did *nothing* to prove that the man in the grave was Jesse James. It only proved that the man originally placed in the grave in 1882 at the original site on the James Farm and then exhumed and reburied in 1902 in Mt. Olivet Cemetery was the same man.

There is no doubt in my mind that Jesse James succeeded in faking his death on April 3, 1882. In fact, he did such a good job of it that it has been difficult for me to get the true story sorted out. I am so grateful that I have the family photographs—undeniable matches for the James family photographs. The photographs have convinced almost everyone who has seen them that I'm right about James L. Courtney and Jesse James being one and the same.

Chapter 7

★　　★　　★

Claims to the James Name

S INCE 1882 MANY PEOPLE have claimed that either they were the real Jesse James or that they are descended from him:

• J. Frank Dalton first claimed he was really Jesse James around 1947. Dalton's great-grandson, Jesse James IV, is represented by former Texas attorney general Waggoner Carr. They support their claim with affidavits from friends and family who heard one of Dalton's many claims to being the famous outlaw. They also have a Hood County autopsy report that identifies Dalton as Jesse Woodson James. The report states that he was missing the tip of his left middle finger (as has been claimed about Jesse James) and had thirty-three or more bullet wounds on his body. But other accounts, including Homer Croy's *Complete and Authentic Life of Jesse James,* have it that Dalton wasn't missing the tip of his finger at all, and that the only thing wrong with his finger was that he had a bent fingernail.

Dalton has also been known to use the surname of Carr (as in Waggoner Carr).

Jesse James IV claims Bob Ford really shot a Missouri outlaw by the name of Charlie Bigelow, not Jesse James; and since everyone believed he was dead, Jesse was able to start a new life in Texas. This enabled the Missouri governor to be reelected because he had kept his reelection promise to stop the James Gang, and it appeared that everyone was happy—except of course, Charlie Bigelow.

Dalton is buried in Granbury, Texas. His tombstone bears the name "Jesse Woodson James."

- Vincel Simmons, from Hughesville, Missouri, believes Jacob Benjamin Gerlt was the real Jesse James. He plans to submit his own blood for testing against the Mitochondrial DNA extracted from the remains exhumed from the claimed grave of Jesse James in 1995. He also plans to exhume Gerlt.

- Allen Crawford claims Jesse Robert James was the man exhumed in Mt. Olivet Cemetery, not Jesse James. He doesn't want to reveal where the man he claims to be Jesse Woodson James, "the one and only," is buried. He's afraid someone will "dig him up." He also wants to see if his story is worth anything to the press or scientists.

- James Ross and Betty Barr claim their great-grandfather was Jesse James. They believe the historically accepted accounts of Jesse James marrying Zee Mimms and fathering her two children. They also believe that Bob Ford actually shot Jesse James and that he is buried in Mt. Olivet Cemetery.

  They wanted the 1995 exhumation of the questioned grave to "silence those claiming some relation to the famous outlaw Jesse James once and for all," as reported in the *Kearney Courier* Special Edition. Ross, a retired judge, has successfully sued three Jesse James impostors and their descendants. The Ross and Barr families are very involved with the James Farm and the James/Younger Gang.

The James Farm was purchased by the Clay County Parks Department and is now a tourist attraction that is visited by people from all over the world. Hundreds of tourists visit the farm daily.

Other Jesse James tourist attractions in Missouri are the

house in St. Joseph where Jesse was allegedly shot, the Jesse James Bank Museum, and the Jesse James Festival that is held annually in Kearney.

Jesse James has probably brought more money to Missouri through all the Jesse James attractions than he ever took out of it. Some who want to be related to him may have that in mind. But my goal is only to get the facts straight. And to give Grandpa back his real name.

Chapter 8

One and the Same

*M*Y GREAT-GRANDFATHER CAME to Texas in 1871. One story has it that he and a bunch of his friends were just riding around having fun and ended up in Texas. But the truth is that he seemed to have a planned destination in mind.

On July 4 he left his friends in Fort Worth and met Thomas Hudson Barron, an early day captain of the Texas Rangers, in Waco, Texas. An interesting item found on an old wanted poster posted by the sheriff of Clay County, Missouri, is that "Cole Younger rode with the Texas Rangers in Waco, Texas." (Another connection between the James Gang and Waco was a surgical operation Frank James had on his leg in Waco after being shot at Northfield, Minnesota.)

Thomas Barron lived in Waco, and then later on moved to the small farming community of Blevins, which is approximately thirty miles southeast of Waco. According to Grandpa's diary, he met Barron in Stephenville and they rode back to Barron's ranch together. Grandpa referred to Barron as the captain, the old gentleman, the old man, and later on as Pa. On October 31, 1871 (October 31 is the same day he gave for his birthdate) my great-grandfather married Barron's daughter, Mary Ellen. They were married thirty-nine years and had eight children.

My father said that Grandpa rode up to the Barron ranch with the saddlebags of his horse and the horse he was leading full of gold.

According to Joseph Rosa's *Age of the Gunfighter,* Jesse James trusted no one and was very suspicious of strangers. The story about Grandpa putting out all the lights when someone would ride up to his house after dark and lying down across the doorway with his pistol cocked fits this description. I'd say being cautious paid off because he lived to be a very old man.

Grandpa purchased a 160-acre tract of farm land from Barron and paid for it free and clear with gold. He also bought every new piece of farm equipment that came onto the market. Rumors still persist in the Blevins area until this very day about the gold and silver Grandpa buried in different places. Grandpa also bought and paid cash for farms for each of his eight children when they married.

My grandmother (Grandpa's daughter, Ida) remembered sitting in her father's front yard visiting with friends. As she talked she was idly poking in the dirt with a stick. Much to her surprise, she unearthed a gallon jar full of gold coins. In another incident, Jewell, her daughter, was making mud pies in Grandpa's front yard and dug up another jar of money. Not only did he have large amounts of money buried, he had five-gallon buckets full of silver dollars sitting around his house and had more than $50,000 in cash in one of his trunks.

How did a man who was supposed to be an ordinary farmer make that kind of money off of a 160-acre farm?

Family history says that Grandpa fought for the Union during the Civil War. But why would a Union man name a favorite pair of his horses John and Reb? Historical accounts show that Frank James posed as a Union man to help conceal his true identity— just as Grandpa did.

Grandpa loved mules and named one of them Buck. That was also the nickname Jesse James gave to his brother Frank.

On the back of an old photograph of Grandpa and his brother they are identified as James L. Courtney and his brother, Fletcher Bagley. Since they both had the same parents, why would one of them have the surname of Courtney and the other Bagley?

It is a fact that Jesse James' mother had been visiting her son Frank James in Fletcher, Oklahoma, when she died on the train on her way back to Missouri. Could Frank James and Fletcher Bagley have been the same man?

My great-grandfather's prowess with a gun was legendary. He could shoot the head off a chicken while riding his horse at full speed. Using his pistol just seemed to come naturally to Grandpa. If he thought a situation called for it, he did not hesitate to use it.

In one incident, "Old Man Clark" (a neighbor) was apparently camped on the wrong side of the creek and had a campfire going. Grandpa rode up and asked Clark to put out the fire because he was afraid of a prairie fire starting due to the dry weather conditions. Clark refused, so Grandpa threw down on him and made him douse the fire. According to family history, Clark turned Grandpa in for carrying a pistol, which was against the law in post-Civil War Texas. There is a claim that Grandpa served nine months in the Falls County Jail, but I have searched the records at the Falls County Courthouse in Marlin and found no records to document the claim.

In another incident Grandpa was riding on his land and rode up on a group of men (headed by a D. W. McGlasson) constructing a fence on his property. Grandpa made them tear down the 1,600 feet of fencing they had built with "force and arms." McGlasson filed charges on Grandpa and a citation was issued by Sheriff Jolly. Two years later, Jolly appointed Grandpa deputy sheriff of Falls County. The sheriff had no idea that the most wanted outlaw in American history was now his deputy. (Outlaws must have made good lawmen, because Jim Younger also became a deputy sheriff in Texas.)

Grandpa Courtney and his new bride, Mary Ellen, hadn't been in their own home long when a band of riders came riding up

★   ★   ★

Grandpa described himself as "Dutch, Irish, and a damn Yankee." Telling people he was a Yankee was part of his cover.

★   ★   ★

late one night. It is believed that the men thought Grandpa was away from home. The men yelled for him to come outside. Mary Ellen called out that he wasn't there. But Grandpa shouted, "I am here and I'll be out as soon as I get my clothes on!" It has been said that the men sensed something in his voice because they left before he could get out there. It is speculated that they knew some of them would have died right then and there if they had waited for Grandpa to appear.

Grandpa belonged to Masonic Lodge #640 in Troy, Texas. A member borrowed money from him and then refused to pay him back. A dispute arose and all agreed to let the Masons arbitrate the matter. Grandpa was accused of saying Masonry was a fraud and was no good and that some men used it as a cloak to hide their meanness. He said he wouldn't believe member Frank Griggs if he was on oath and he wouldn't believe another member, D. M. McGlasson, under any circumstances. McGlasson was accused of swindling $200 out of him and Grandpa said that he would have rather they had broken into his house and stolen it. Grandpa also called his brethren "grand rascals" because they were trying to swindle, cheat, and defraud him out of his just rights. Clark accused Grandpa of gross, un-Masonic conduct not proper enough to be written. Family history has it that Grandpa threw down on the men. It is believed—no surprise—that the Masons ruled against Grandpa.

In another incident between Frank Griggs and Grandpa, Griggs rode over to Grandpa's house and invited him to a barbecue to make peace, or so he said. Grandpa agreed to go and they rode to a place in the country. When they dismounted Grandpa threw down on Griggs and told him to tell his boys to come out from behind the trees. Griggs' boys were in fact there, hiding behind the trees. Grandpa was sure they had planned an ambush to kill him, and I believe he was right.

Even though Grandpa had rough ways, he was a Christian. At a birthday party for one of Grandpa's daughters the guests played records on an old Victrola and danced. When the Deer Creek Baptist Church found out about their merrymaking, they turned Grandpa out of the church. He continued going to revivals, but had to stand outside to hear the preaching.

Jesse James was the son of a preacher and is said to have had strong religious beliefs.

> *According to the Waco Baptist Association's published proceedings, 1884, Grandpa was a delegate sent by Deer Creek Baptist Church to the Waco Convention.*
>
> *After he was "turned out" of the church he would say he was "going to see the preacher," which meant he was going to his locked whiskey cabinet to get a drink.*

There was a dispute between W. M. Teel and Grandpa over Grandpa's teenaged second wife, Edna Henry, whom he married in 1915 (five years after my great-grandmother, Mary Ellen, died). Grandpa was sixty-nine years old. The following letters were found in Grandpa's personal belongings after his death:

Mr. Courtney

We have told you to take your wife away before she get in to troble but you won't and so we or telling you one more time and if you don't you going to get in to troble your self we don't want to see your wife get in to troble so that the reason were writing to you and we no that she will if you don't send her away untill ever thing get write so you better heed our warning if you don't take your wife away thir going to burn your house up why don't you carrie her away for a while until things get straight

a friend

Grandpa's response to the request to get rid of Edna Henry Courtney was as follows:

W. M. Teel

Your time is come you better get your hat and get out if you don't you will smell hell your bunch has ruined a good family now the people is going to see that you have to leave if you don't get out the good people will blow you to hell and burn everything

you have and so it in Johnson grass now we have seen them children run bare ass we can stand now hell is behind this [story]
stay if you want to but your ass will be blown up this aint no bluff
if you think it is gist stay and see we don't want to kill no body
you better get busy hell is to pay hell be with you.

"Sind the people"
This August the 27=1916

Grandpa was known for having no fear of anyone or anything. Just like Jesse James.

The marriage between Edna and Grandpa did not last.
According to oral family history she wasn't too bright, and after an
incident where she almost suffocated one of Grandpa's grandchildren he is said to have bought her a lot of clothes and dolls and
sent her back home. He also purchased a house and a lot for her
family in East Texas. But he never succeeded in getting rid of the
Henrys; they are said to have popped in and out of his life until he
died.

In 1919 Grandpa married Ollie Nelson. She was also much
younger than Grandpa, but the story goes that she was a good wife
and stayed with him until he died.

It seemed to be the same group of men—Griggs, McGlasson,
and Clark—that Grandpa continued to have problems with. Some
of Grandpa's problems probably stemmed from his claiming to be
a Yankee to help conceal his true identity. It couldn't have been
easy living as a northerner in a Confederate state so soon after the
Civil War. The wounds were still too fresh.

My great-grandfather had revealed the truth about his true
identity to my grandmother and she in turn told her children.
When Grandpa died, the contents of his trunk were divided
between several of his children. Included in his trunk were photographs, hundreds of personal letters, tax receipts, diaries, documents, and the clothes he was wearing when he died. These items
have been passed down from one generation to the next. Many of
the items were destroyed when a cousin burned them, for what she
claimed was for the goodwill of the family.

In a letter from Aunt Irene (my father's sister) dated February
22, 1973, to a cousin, she wrote that Grandpa was born in Kansas
City (Jesse James was born a few miles northeast of Kansas City).

> ★   ★   ★
>
> *Grandpa's brother-in-law wrote that*
> *Grandpa never talked about his father*
> *and mother, but said he lived as a neighbor*
> *to Jesse and Frank James.*
>
> ★   ★   ★

The letter also stated that Grandpa fought for the South and that he was only sixteen when he joined the army (Jesse James joined the army at the age of sixteen). Aunt Irene also hinted about the family secret of Grandpa really being Jesse James in the letter.

Grandpa was said to have tried for years and was finally successful in getting a pension for serving in the Union Army. Somehow he was able to erase a desertion charge and was able to convince the army he was James L. Courtney.

A James L. Courtney did serve in the Union Army as a bugler in Co. M under a Captain Smith. Courtney enlisted on January 14, 1864, in Warrensburg, Missouri, at the age of eighteen and is described as 5'10 with dark hair and blue eyes. (Relatives who knew Grandpa describe him as around 6'4 or 6'5 and having medium blond hair with blue eyes.) James L. Courtney deserted the army at Columbus, North Carolina, on August 21, 1865. My great-grandfather was not James L. Courtney. James L. Courtney was his alias.

Grandpa kept meticulous records of births, deaths, money earned and spent, and even recorded the date and time he saw the first "flying machine" fly over his house. He kept these records for most of his life. Knowing this, I found it strange when I read a letter from Captain Smith responding to a letter he had received from Grandpa. (Smith fought for the Union.) Grandpa had obviously written to Smith asking for dates and locations of different battles that his company participated in during the Civil War. Captain Smith seemed to think it was strange that Grandpa didn't remember the dates because he made the following comment: "All of us who were in that battle will remember the day and the date." Smith gave Grandpa many names, dates, and locations of battles—

18|

12 .... Reg't Cav. Vols.

Courtney James Age........

Rank........ *Pvt, Bug'r Co. M*

Captain........ *Smith,*

Enlisted........ *Jan, 4* ...186 4

Where........ *Warrensburg Mo*

Mustered in........ *Mar, 16* 186 4

Where........ *B, Brks, Mo,*

Remarks *Dis'd, Aug,*
21, 65, By order
of Sec of War,

....

....

....

Mustered out........................186 ...

Where..

Form No. 242, A. G. O., Mo., 11-3-11-18M

MISSOURI STATE ARCHIVES
CERTIFICATE OF WAR SERVICE
Union

4-83

Name as: J. L.
18
5'10"
Dark
Blue
Light
Single
Farmer
Nat: Washington, Tenn.
Place: Warrensburg,
Johnson Co, Mo,
Rem: Deserted at
Columbus, North Carolina
Aug 21, 1865.

Certificate of war service (Union Army) for James L. Courtney. Grandpa tried for years to get these records and receive a pension from the government—once again duping the Yankees.

Keytesville, Mo., _____ 1899

In regard to the fight in which our horses were captured—
I was not in that fight   I was there laying in Hospital
at Memphis Tenn—   I joined the command at Edgfull
Tenn — before the Battle of Nashville — which commenced on
the morning of the 15th day of December 1864.
All of us who were in that will remember — the day — and the date.

I was left in the woods to die near White Station Tenn. about the
5th of Sept 1864. They left old Cummins & Sandy Botts to bury me
but forgot to leave them any spades to dig a grave with. and
the boys concluded they would get me into Memphis Tenn
to a Hospital which they did in time to save my life — and the
result is I am on hands yet.   I remained in the Hospital
51 days. and got out in time to take a hand in the fight at Nashv.
and from there on down to Columbia Tenn — where I
broke down again Dec 22 1864 — and sent back to Edgfield.

I have always understood that the fight in which our Co rathers lost
their horses was near Campbellsville in Tenn., in November 18
Our Regiment was part of Gen Edward Hatchs Cav command — covering the
retreat of Gen Geo H Thomas into Nashville — and had to

The letter which Captain Smith wrote to Grandpa gave him all the information he needed to request a pension.

enough for him to finally succeed in getting the pension he was seeking. Jesse James was still getting his revenge by taking money from the very government he fought against.

When I first started researching Grandpa, I was confused because the family claimed he was born in Tennessee on October 31, 1846, and that he was Stephen and Dianah Courtney's first child. But according to the 1850 federal census records for Jefferson County, Tennessee, there was no James L. Courtney listed as the first child of Stephen and Dianah Courtney. Only one child was listed in the Courtney household, a girl by the name of Harriet. A thirty-year-old woman by the name of Sarah Sitrell was also listed as living in the Courtney household.

Where was James L. Courtney? He would have been over three years old. No parent would forget to list one of their children, much less their first-born son, but remember to list a woman who wasn't even a family member.

The federal census records for 1860 show that the Courtneys were living in Post Oak Township, Johnson County, Missouri, which is approximately forty miles from the farm where Jesse James and his family lived. This is when James L. Courtney mysteriously appeared listed as the oldest child of Stephen and Dianah Courtney.

I believe this is the time Jesse W. James first assumed the name of James L. Courtney, a name he would use off and on for the rest of his life.

Jesse's family and other Southern sympathizers had already experienced trouble with the Kansas Red Legs; with the trouble rapidly escalating, Jesse may have been sent to the home of the Jameses' friends and neighbors, the Courtneys, to get him out of harm's way. Zerelda, being very vocal about her Southern sympathies, seemed to bring unwanted attention from groups like the Red Legs who had opposing views.

There was a James L. Courtney who fought for the Union Army. He was listed as a deserter on his military records. My theory is that he may not have deserted, but may have been killed by the Rebs. It has been reported that the Rebs would search the uniforms and personal belongings found on dead Union soldiers in order to identify them. This may have been how Jesse assumed the identity of the real James L. Courtney. Several tombstones in Mt. Olivet Cemetery bear the name of James L. Courtney. Then again,

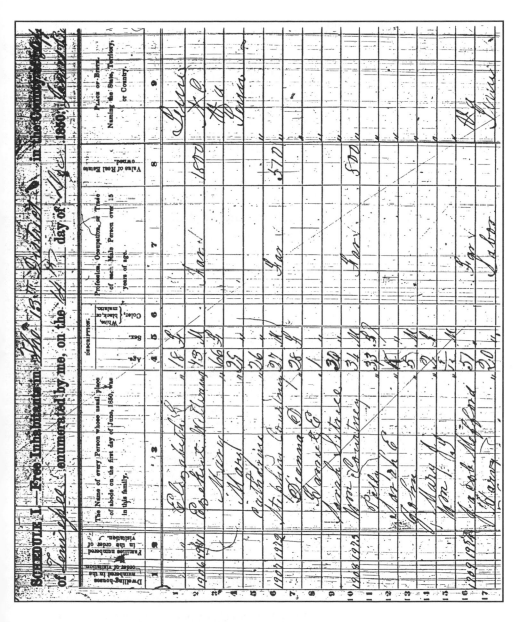

1850 Jefferson County TN Census. There is no James L. Courtney listed as being the oldest child of Stephen and Dianah Courtney.

he may have known that a James Courtney had died, and assumed his identity.

I have not found any information among my great-grandfather's belongings to document exactly how he chose his alias, but I do know the James family had a close connection to the Courtneys. Jesse's father, Reverend Robert James, baptized and married several members of the Courtney family, and several Courtneys lived in Clay County near the James farm.

Because Jesse James was well acquainted with the Courtneys it is logical that he used the Courtney name as his alias. The authorities had such varied descriptions of Jesse James, he could just blend in and pretend to be a Courtney without raising any suspicions.

Around 1864 the Courtneys moved from Johnson County, Missouri, to Miami County, Kansas. They may have moved to escape the turmoil of war which had gotten too close for comfort. Confederate General Sterling Price and his army of men were in Johnson County at that time in what is now known as Price's Raid. Another reason the Courtneys may have moved was to escape the militia that was trying to track down the Confederate guerrillas with which Jesse and Frank fought.

Sometime late in 1865 the Courtneys seemed to vanish from the public record. I had heard from family members that this family may have moved to a surrounding state and changed their names. After exhausting the Missouri census records, I tried Kansas. Only by going through the 1870 Kansas census records one name at a time did I discover that the Courtneys not only had a new residence, but they had new identities as well. Stephen Courtney had become Andrew Jackson Haun, and Dianah, James L., and the rest of the family kept their given names and only changed their surname to Haun. They now resided in Morris County, Kansas.

The Courtney (Haun) family had to feel seriously threatened to go to such extremes to hide. Oral family history has it that the Courtneys changed their name to Haun because James L. deserted the Union Army during the war and that they were so ashamed the entire family changed their names and hid for the rest of their lives. Another version, which I believe is correct, is that James L. (Jesse James) was in some serious trouble and had to go to Texas to escape.

The front of J. L. Courtney's diary, where he wrote "in case of death" instructions.

I suspect that the Courtney (Haun) family had to change their name and hide forever because someone probably became suspicious of James L. Courtney, his companions, and their activities.

In the 1880 census records for Morris County, Kansas, a James Wilkerson was listed as a member of the Courtney aka Haun household. James Wilkerson was a known James Gang member. Bill Wilkerson, James' brother, is mentioned in Grandpa's diary and was also a member of the James Gang.

A young man by the name of Howard Carr from Ohio was also living with the Hauns. J. Frank Dalton, who later claimed to be Jesse James, went under the name of Carr at one time. It intrigues me that Dalton did not claim to be Jesse James until 1947 —after my great-grandfather died in 1943. Could J. Frank Dalton have been Howard Carr? That would explain how Dalton acquired the facts he knew about Jesse James.

When Grandpa started for Texas he again assumed the surname of Courtney. He wrote inside the front cover of the diary that he purchased in Decatur, Texas: "if the oner, James L. Courtney, should be found dead the person he finds this will please rite immediately to E. L. [Erastus, "Rat"] Lafayette Andruss Brosley PO Cass Co. Mo." (Incidentally, Decatur, Texas, was a favorite camping spot of Frank and Jesse James.)

Why would Grandpa list his uncle as the person to be notified in case of his death if the Courtneys aka Hauns were truly his parents? Stephen Courtney aka Andrew Jackson Haun did not die until 1882, and Dianah didn't die until 1917, so they were both living when Grandpa was making his trip to Texas. I believe it was because Grandpa couldn't have put his real mother or stepfather's name in his diary in the event that someone else may have read it and discovered his true identity.

According to Courtney/Haun family history, there was very little contact with James L. after he left Kansas in 1871 and made Texas his new home. But, according to my grandmother and Grandpa's diary, he was always sending letters back home. It was just that the Courtneys (Hauns) weren't his parents and the letters sent "back home" went to Missouri and Zerelda Samuel, not Kansas.

There are several items showing a strong connection between the James/Samuel and Courtney families that would explain why Jesse James would choose the Courtney name for his alias:

- An affidavit is displayed at the James Farm Museum in Kearney that is signed by an A. J. Courtney (a neighbor to Reuben and Zerelda Samuel) trying to get Reuben Samuel released from jail in St. Joseph.
- There are at least ten tombstones bearing the Courtney name surrounding the burial places of Zerelda, Dr. Samuel, and their son Archie in the small Mt. Olivet Cemetery in Kearney.
- Still another Courtney connection was the former sheriff of Clay County, W. J. Courtney, who served Pinkerton Detective J. W. Whicher his last meal on earth.
- Many members of the Courtney family were married or baptized by Reverend James (Jesse's father).

The *Pioneer Times,* a quarterly publication of the Mid-Missouri Genealogical Society, added further connections in an October 1985 (Vol. 9, No. 4) article. Included is quoted information from Wilrena Calvert Miller:

"The COURTNEY land in Clay County was near the home of Rev. Robert James, father of Frank and Jesse James. You will note in the obituary of Mrs. Josephus COURTNEY that Mrs. Frank James came from Missouri to Kansas for the funeral. . . .

"Our family said that Jesse James' mother could do beautiful embroidery despite the loss of part of one arm, lost in the tragedy (bomb) at the time Jesse's little brother (Archie Samuel) was killed, 26 Jan. 1875.

"I was told she would place the fabric over the stub to do her stitches; so it would appear the arm was lost at the elbow or below.

"Aunt Pets' nephew, Jack Dootson says his mother Mary remembers Frank James coming to their place to borrow a plow."

In the same publication, this paragraph is found:

Notes from the Liberty Tribune tell of Robert James and wife who came to Clay County in 1842, the same year that he was ordained to Preach by the Baptist, at Old New Hope. The next year Frank James was born (1843) and Jesse James in 1847. Robert James preached until 1850 when he went to California.

Under him, Jos. courtney and his wife joined the Church. "There was no better man than Robert James."

It is evident that Jesse was very familiar with the Courtneys, which was a wise thing to do if he was passing himself off as one of the family.

Grandpa used coded messages frequently when writing in his diary and in drawing his treasure maps. For example, "the 46d 718 g3ve h3s c4s28t f49 t4 h1ve 26628" translates to "the old man give his consent for me to have Ellen."

The James Gang also used coded messages they learned as Partisan Rangers during the Civil War when corresponding with one another.

On June 3, 1871, Grandpa made the following entry in his diary: "Monday morning in camp at Elizabeth[town] and started for Fort Worth and traveled 10 mile and camped on the big focel and then traveled into town

for eggs 15
for melon 25
for sugar 50
for soda 10
for horse shewing 100

and then went down on the (marked out) clear fork and camped and at nite moved camp 2 mile in the country the distance was 20 m."

According to Homer Croy's *Jesse James Was My Neighbor,* Jesse James would make camp and then after dark move to a different location miles away. This was done as a precautionary measure in the event someone was following him. Grandpa apparently did the same.

In nearly every historical account written about Jesse James, an eye affliction is mentioned. The symptoms were an unusual amount of blinking. This same blinking problem exists in different members of my family. Medical doctors usually attribute the problem to allergies.

During our meeting at the James Farm, George Warfel noticed a white mole in the crease of my nose and cheek and asked

★   ★   ★

When Grandpa left his house for any
reason, he would leave in one direction
and always come back in a different
direction. Also, when Grandpa would
take money to bury someplace, not one
of his family dared to follow him to try
and see where he buried it because they
were too afraid of what the conse-
quences would be if he caught them.

★   ★   ★

if I knew that they were genetic and ran in the James family. He said that Zerelda had a white mole in the same location as mine.

I asked my dermatologist, Dr. Eugene Schoch, if white moles are genetic. He confirmed that they are and said that M. D. Anderson Hospital has done studies on moles. They found one particular family where the women all had moles in the same location on their chins.

Maybe the answer has been right under my nose all along.

Chapter 9

Getting Things Straight

*I*N MY OPINION THERE have been many incorrect reports made concerning Jesse James. Some of them are as follows:

1. His size—Nearly every written account has it that Jesse James' height was anywhere from 5'9 to 5'11 and that he had a "gracile" body build. But according to John N. Edwards' *Noted Guerrillas,* "His form—tall and finely moulded—was capable of great effort and great endurance. . . . Looking at the small, white hands with their long, tapering fingers, it was not written or recorded that they were to become with a revolver among the quickest and deadliest hands in the west."

My great-grandfather was said to be a giant of a man standing at least 6'4 tall with a large bone structure and a lean, muscular build.

After a train robbery at Gads Hill, Missouri, on January 31, 1874, Jesse James handed the conductor a note that partially described the gang. The note read: "The robbers were all large men, none under six feet tall."

Jesse James' mother stood six feet tall and had a large bone structure. His father appeared to be a tall man in the portrait I saw of him. It is likely that Jesse James would take after his parents.

2. His marriage—History reports that Jesse married his first

70

cousin Zee Mimms in April of 1874. There is no marriage license proving the marriage ever existed and no census records proving that Jesse James and Zee Mimms were husband and wife.

My great-grandfather married Mary Ellen Barron on October 31, 1871. Entries in his diary tell of going to Marlin, Texas, to buy a marriage license and new clothes for the wedding. He even listed the purchase price of each item. Though I have searched for the marriage license at the Falls County Courthouse, I have been unable to locate it. Personnel there say it may have been lost or stolen when the originals were available to the public, or my great-grandparents may have failed to have it recorded. But it is documented in Grandpa's diary that he did purchase a marriage license in Marlin, Texas, at the Falls County Courthouse.

3. His children—Jesse is claimed to be the father of Zee's son and daughter. The claim is that he had assumed the name of Thomas Howard, and that his son was named Tim Howard at birth. At a later date, Tim Howard called himself Jesse Edwards James. I believe Wood Hite (Jesse's first cousin) and Thomas Howard were the same person, and therefore those who were born to Thomas Howard were not the children of Jesse James.

My great-grandparents (James and Mary Ellen) had eight children: two sons and six daughters.

4. His handwriting—Some of the letters claimed to have been written by Jesse James were actually written by journalist John Newman Edwards. This was documented by T. J. Stiles, who wrote *Jesse James*.

During the James boys' outlaw years, Edwards proved to be a loyal friend by writing letters proclaiming their innocence and publishing them in newspapers. Edwards signed these handwritten letters "Jesse James." I believe that the letters written by Edwards and signed "Jesse James" have been used as authentic samples of Jesse James' handwriting.

Anyone who challenges the Ross/Barr group is asked to submit samples of their contender's handwriting for comparison to handwriting that they claim is the authentic handwriting of Jesse James.

It has been reported that Jesse had labored, child-like handwriting. Where are these letters? When I requested copies of these letters from the James Farm I was told that only one letter written by Jesse James existed. It did not appear labored or child-like in any way and was signed "Tho. Howard." Yet, while watching "In Search of Jesse James," the A&E documentary of the 1995 exhumation of the purported grave of Jesse James, different letters were displayed that were claimed to have been written by Jesse. The letters had columns of figures that appeared very similar to columns of figures in Grandpa's diary where he kept an account of his money. It's possible that letters written by Grandpa to his mother (Zerelda) were found in her belongings after her death, and if so the Ross/Barr group or the James Farm would be in possession of those now.

I have requested copies of the letters shown in the documentary from George Warfel but have not received them at this date. He said that some letters had been copyrighted and that those couldn't be released.

I don't believe handwriting should be a deciding factor in determining who the real Jesse James was for this reason: Either the James Farm doesn't have authentic samples of Jesse's writing or they will not share it.

5. Places of residence—I agree with historical accounts of Jesse being born in Kearney, Missouri, and living on the farm until he was a teenager. I do not agree with accounts that Jesse resided in Tennessee in 1875 through 1880. My great-grandfather was born in Missouri but made Texas his home in 1871. I certainly don't agree that he was living in St. Joseph, Missouri, in 1882.

6. Photographs—In my opinion many of the photographs that are claimed to be authentic photographs of Jesse James are not him at all. I believe the most famous photograph of Jesse James is authentic because the internationally noted forensic artist that examined my photographs indicated that the features of my great-grandfather and the features of Jesse James (in the most famous photograph) are consistent.

It doesn't take an expert to see that many of the photos Warfel claims to be Jesse do not match the most famous photo of Jesse James. (See *The Many Faces of Jesse James* by Phillip Steele and George Warfel.)

Warfel is a very good portrait artist, but he is not a forensic artist, and readily admits that he doesn't have the same level of expertise that those in state law enforcement have. I would guess that photographs submitted to Warfel for his opinion of their authenticity have a much better chance of being considered genuine if the remitter is not claiming to be a descendant of the James family or disputing the historically accepted story of Jesse James.

Any person outside of the group in Missouri who challenges their claim of who is really in the grave is told to have their photographs examined by someone on the level of the state police. Why shouldn't their photographs be subjected to the same level of scrutiny?

7. Personal habits—Historians have written that Jesse James was a gambler and died broke. That couldn't be further from the truth. Grandpa worked hard on his farm every day and was financially secure when he died. He helped family and friends financially, and it has been said that he would give anyone one chance. But if they blew it, that was it—he was through with them.

For Grandpa to keep detailed records of every penny earned and spent shows that he valued money too much to just gamble it away.

It has also been claimed that Jesse James didn't smoke or drink. Those who knew Grandpa said he did not use tobacco, but he did drink on occasion, and kept cases of whiskey under his bed for medicinal purposes. Grandpa believed that if you were sick you either needed a shot of whiskey or a "dose of medicine" (laxative), or both, if one or the other didn't work. He also drank on occasion for non-medicinal purposes.

8. Jesse James' death—On April 3, 1882, the *Kansas City Journal* reported that Bob Ford shot Jesse James (aka Thomas Howard) in the head, shattering the skull. There was a wound reported over his eye that at the time was thought to be where the bullet exited.

His wife and children were said to have lined up to view Jesse's body. A coroner's inquest was held and an autopsy performed. Zerelda, Zee Mimms, ex-Ranger comrades, fellow gang members, and the sheriff of Clay County (Sheriff Timberlake) all confirmed that the corpse was indeed Jesse James.

When I told Warfel and Steele I didn't believe that Jesse James was shot dead by Bob Ford, or anyone else, Warfel asked, why would his wife and children cry and wail if it wasn't Jesse James? I told him that they were crying and wailing over the death of their husband and father but that didn't mean he was Jesse James. Steele asked why all those spectators would line up to view the body if it wasn't Jesse James. My answer to that was that all those people were told it was Jesse James, and that very few people actually had his description. That's one reason he was never caught.

According to a special dispatch to the *Kansas City Journal* on April 6, 1882, Coroner Richard Bohanon, acting on a tip, retrieved the body of Wood Hite from Bob Ford's farm. I find it ironic that Hite's body just happened to be found on the very night that an autopsy was being performed on the purported head of Jesse James. Even more ironic is that the coroner's description of Hite's wounds appeared to be identical to the coroner's description of the wounds on the purported body of Jesse James—both shot in the head, shattered skulls, and wounds over an eye. The coroner did describe a slight wound on Hite's right arm that was not described on Jesse's arm, but what is suspicious is that a slight wound appears to be on the purported body of Jesse James in a photo picturing him in a coffin (T. J. Stiles, *Jesse James*, 103). Even more intriguing is the fact that Hite was shot dead by Bob Ford, the same man who reportedly killed Jesse.

Bob Ford's sister, Martha Bolton, testified that Hite and Dick Liddil got in a gunfight over her affections and had only succeeded in wounding one another when her brother Bob suddenly just decided to shoot Hite in the head, killing him. The shooting supposedly happened in December of 1881. Both Bolton and Liddil had met with Missouri's Governor Crittenden about aiding him in capturing Jesse James in December of 1881.

It's apparent to me from this and other evidence that there were never two bodies. Jesse James was not shot dead on April 3, 1882, but I believe Wood Hite was and was purposely identified as Jesse James. You can see for yourself that the similarities seem more than just coincidental. The slight wound reported to be on Hite's right arm is an identifying mark and it helps tell the tale of who was really pictured in the coffin and who is really buried in Mt. Olivet Cemetery under the name Jesse Woodson James.

A Winchester rifle, model 1873, owned by Wood Hite and

marked with the initials W. H. (Wood Hite) and T. H. (Thomas Howard—purportedly the alias of Jesse James) provides strong evidence that Wood Hite and Thomas Howard were probably the same man. There is no way to prove that Jesse James used the alias of Thomas Howard.

Zerelda, Zee Mimms, Ranger comrades, fellow gang members and Sheriff Timberlake (who was a friend of the James family) would probably not have hesitated to falsely identify Wood Hite as Jesse James for the obvious reason of giving Jesse a chance to start a new life. They all had close connections to him.

Whether Hite was intentionally killed by Bob Ford to help Jesse start a new life is not known by any living person, but the circumstances surrounding Hite's death and the purported death of Jesse provide good evidence for the possibility of a switch.

A strange incident happened to me recently. I was at a mail center in Cedar Park, Texas, having some copies made. The clerk had asked how my book about Jesse James was coming along when I noticed a man standing nearby jerk his head up. She then asked if I had seen a documentary on TV about Jesse not really being in the grave in Missouri. I told her I hadn't seen it, but that I certainly agreed with what they were saying. The man spoke up and said his last name was Ford and that he was a descendant of Bob Ford. He said it had been passed down in his family that Jesse James was not the man Bob Ford shot and that James was not buried in that grave.

Needless to say, I was surprised by this encounter. I introduced myself and explained that I believe my great-grandfather was Jesse James and that I would love to hear more of his story. He refused, saying that his family wasn't exactly proud of Bob Ford. I told him that since Bob Ford didn't shoot Jesse James in the back of the head, it was his chance to help clear his ancestor's name. He looked me straight in the eye and said he knew that Ford didn't shoot Jesse James in the back of the head, but he *did* shoot someone in the back of the head, and in his book that made him a coward.

We both went our separate ways, but I still think of that meeting. What would the odds be on descendants of Bob Ford and

Jesse James being in the same place at the same time and talking about an incident that involved their relatives more than a century ago?

On February 23, 1996, James Starrs claimed that the 1995 exhumation proved with a 99.7 degree of certainty that the man in the questioned grave was a direct descendant of Zerelda Samuel and that Jesse James is buried in that grave. I do not believe Jesse James is in that grave. My great-grandfather is buried in Blevins Cemetery in Texas.

I can understand why so many people believe that Bob Ford shot and killed Jesse James and that he is buried in Mt. Olivet Cemetery in Missouri. After all, they are believing just what Jesse wanted them to believe or he would never have been able to pull off one of the biggest bluffs in American history.

This would not be the first time Jesse tried to fake his death. In 1879 gang member George Shepard reported to authorities that he had shot Jesse in the back of the head at Shoal Creek, Missouri (again they claimed he was shot in the back of the head) and dumped his body in the creek. When the authorities investigated and found no body, Shepard's claim was considered to be a hoax.

Interestingly, Grandpa used to mail letters back home to Shoal Creek, Missouri.

Chapter 10

★　　★　　★

Life in Texas

RANDPA AND MY GREAT-GRANDMOTHER Mary Ellen lived with her parents for a couple of years, and Grandpa soon became Mr. Barron's right-hand man. I believe this caused some trouble with Barron's sons because they were jealous of my great-grandfather's relationship with their father. Barron thought very highly of him.

He was a huge man and seemed to have unlimited energy. Some days he would cut at least six acres of hay and then go to a party and dance all night. He and Mary Ellen were very much in love and having the time of their lives.

The Barrons had a large home and there was always a crowd there: Capt. Thomas and Mrs. Barron (Mary Jane), Mary Ellen (whom family members called Ellen) and Grandpa, and many of the Barrons' other children. Thomas Barron had twenty children —twelve with his first wife and eight with my great-great-grandmother, Mary Jane.

Eli, Willie, Maxey, Babe, and Wat (the hired hands) and Harriet (the wash woman) all lived on the Barron place. Overnight visitors were always welcome at the Barrons' house.

Someone Grandpa called "The Thing" was there a few days. I haven't been able to find out who "The Thing" was.

With such a large family living near each other they were

bound to get on each other's nerves at times. Grandpa wrote on January 25, 1872, about Serena (Ellen's sister) marrying Mr. Reid: "all of them remained in the house all day and done nothing, but Bud and Paw and I built fires all day for the rest to quarrel over."

After a revival at the Barrons' home, Grandpa wrote:

"Parson Taylor went home this morning and we done nothing all day only went to look for beaf and Paw whipped Serena and made them move to Reids." (The Reids were Serena Barron's in-laws.)

My great-grandparents went to "rites" most every Sunday and they often held prayer meetings in their home. Preachers were frequent visitors to the Barron place.

Those years were full of hard work and challenge, but Grandpa was young and strong; his Missouri heritage had prepared him for the hardships of Texas.

The men had to search for their horses nearly every day because the brush fences didn't hold them very well; they always needed mending. Barbed wire wasn't being used at that time. Pole corrals made from cedar cut in the cedar brakes were used instead.

Stock ran free for many years after Grandpa came to Texas, and he and the other men caught the mavericks and wild horses and branded them. Wat, the black horse breaker, branded Captain Barron's livestock. Wat had remained with Captain Barron after the Civil War and became a hired hand. Grandpa recorded the brands for everyone.

HK was one of the Courtney brands, a symbol for High Kickers. A joined JB was his other brand. I got chills when I learned that he used that brand. My husband is an artist and has signed his work for years using a joined JB for Joe-Betty. I realize now that this brand may have stood for James-Barron (his last name and her last name).

One night Grandpa and the Barron men were camping after spending the day rounding up strays, when a group of men rode up and asked permission to come into the camp. Permission was granted and the men rode in. They said that Grandpa and the Barron men had some of their cattle and they wanted them back. Grandpa and the Barrons let the men have the cattle they claimed were theirs and trouble was avoided.

After a few years of rounding up and branding cattle, they had a big cattle drive to Kansas and sold the herd there.

There was a constant need for wood; it was cut year-round for the cookstove and the fireplaces they used for warmth when cold blue northers howled across Texas. Hay was cut and stacked, wells dug by hand, and the spring by the house had to be cleaned out. Land was cleared and the brush not used for fences had to be burned.

One day Grandpa was mending a brush fence when he got into a hornet nest. One stung him on the back, and he wrote that the pain was so severe in his back and legs that he could barely stand.

A huge garden was planted with many varieties of vegetables including Indian corn, sweet potatoes, beans, onions, turnips, and watermelons. They had to constantly hoe the garden to keep the weeds from taking over. Fruit trees were planted along with different types of grapes. Grandpa would help Ellen and her sisters cut the peaches for drying them for later use.

When hogs and cattle were butchered, Grandpa would set out the wine he made from the grapevines for everyone to drink. He even used the animal hides for furniture and clothes; what they didn't use they "grained" and sold.

Grandpa wore buckskin pants sometimes because he wrote in his diary: "October 31, 1872—Mary [Mrs. Barron] finished my buckskin pants today."

He went "a huntin" for deer and wild turkey and for bee trees. He loved honey. He kept a honey pot on his dining table, and

★   ★   ★

Grandpa was an avid beekeeper and had over a hundred hives. During World War I a rumor spread around the area that he had money hidden in some of the hives. The funny thing is that the only thing he had hidden in them was sugar.

★   ★   ★

when he was finished eating he would take a spoonful of honey to top off the meal. A syrup mill was built in the creek so that they had syrup for themselves and syrup to sell.

Grandpa bought every new piece of farm implement that came onto the market: hay balers, grain drills, reapers, and pea and corn shellers. The corn he shelled was taken to Cego to be ground into corn meal.

He made his own shingles and also made singletrees.

All of the huge foundation stones for his houses, chimneys, and barns were quarried from west of what is now Interstate Highway 35 by himself. No one knows how he loaded them onto his wagon because they were so heavy.

He loved to fish and had all kinds of fishing equipment, including large fish nets.

Grandpa was a man of many talents. He even surveyed land. He kept detailed records of money earned and spent, births, deaths, and even the weather.

On top of all the work he did he also belonged to several fraternal organizations, including the Improved Order of Red Men, the Masons, and the Good Samaritans. He was on the Commissioners Court and the school board and was a delegate sent by the Little Deer Creek Baptist Church to the Waco Baptist Association in 1884.

According to an elderly cousin, Grandpa was a medium blond with blue eyes. She described his moustache as freshly blackened, and in photographs his hair does appear dark. Historians have written that Jesse James darkened his hair.

★   ★   ★

Not only was Grandpa intelligent, he had a lot of common sense. He could figure out the exact amount of lumber needed to build a new barn or house, and have only scraps left over. He was said to be very good at math, adding columns of figures very fast in his head.

★   ★   ★

Mary Ellen had dark hair and eyes, and was of Native American heritage. Relatives have described their children as having "Indian features" and "Indian ways."

On Saturday, August 10, Grandpa went to get a Mrs. Baker for Ellen. She stayed a week, but the baby they had expected to arrive had not appeared. They took Mrs. Baker home but they soon went for her again, and on August 16, 1872, Mary Dianah (Anah) was born. He wrote in his diary, "The first girl was borned" and paid Mrs. Baker $5.00. He hired one of Ellen's sisters to look after Ellen while she was convalescing and paid her $2.50.

When Louisa was born on August 29, 1874, Mr. Shelton attended Ellen. She was at Ma's (Mrs. Barron's) when the baby came. Grandpa wrote, "She gave birth to a fine girl."

The eight children of Grandpa and Mary Ellen are discussed as follows:

Mary Dianah Courtney (Anah) was born August 16, 1872, and married Lorenzo Dow Patterson. They moved to Haskell County, Texas, and lived on Grandpa's farm when they first married.

Louisa Ellen Courtney was born on August 30, 1874, and married Bradley P. Busby. They had seven children: Albert, Nora, Myrtle, Emma Ruth, Josephine, Clyde, and Annette. They, too, got their start on Grandpa's farm. Later he bought them a farm at Sagerton, Texas, where the children grew up as prominent members of the Segerton Baptist Church. At one time a preacher asked the congregation to look around and see of those present who had the most influence for good in their lives and then go and stand by that person. It was said that the whole congregation went and stood by Louisa.

It has been said that Brad Busby was not much of a farmer. Grandpa always visited once a year, and he said it was strange to him that a German man on one side of the fence had a good crop every year and Brad Busby only made a crop sometimes. The couple moved back to Grandpa's farm when they grew old.

Lillie Jane Courtney was born December 2, 1877. She married Joe Yarborough and they had four children: Thomas (died of flu in World War I), Leslie, Dora, and Opal. They got their start on Grandpa's farm. The family then moved to Arlington.

James William Courtney was born January 11, 1879, and married Emma Lee Mayfield. They had five sons: Jim, Noah, Melvin, Marion, and Byron C. Courtney. They, like so many of the others, started their married life on Grandpa's farm. Grandpa bought them a farm in Stamford, Texas.

Ida Florence Courtney, my grandmother, was born April 5, 1882 (just three days after Jesse James was reported dead). She married William James (Bill) Dorsett and they had eight children: Mary Pearl, Rhoda Edna, Grace Irene, Jewel Isabell, Robert Lafayette (Bud), Jesse Willard (Lit), Opal Lenora, and Howard William (Boy).

Ida met Bill when he was camped on Deer Creek. He was a farm laborer and had hired out to work for Grandpa. Bill has been described as being brutally handsome, and it wasn't long before he and the tall, auburn-haired Ida fell in love.

The trouble was that my great-grandfather thought that Ida could do better for herself and forbade them to see each other. But she had a mind of her own and eloped with Bill. When Grandpa found out that his daughter had run off with his hired hand, he was furious. He hitched up his best team of horses and went after her. He killed those horses by running them so hard, but didn't catch up with the runaways. I guess they had too much of a headstart on him.

I can't help but laugh when I think of what Bill would have done if he had known that Jesse James was hot on his trail and out for blood! Grandpa may have secretly admired him because he probably would have done the same thing.

My grandparents lived most of their married lives in a covered wagon, and some of their children were born in it.

Daddy used to keep a cage full of banty hens hooked under the wagon while they traveled. Mama said he had those chickens trained because anytime they camped for the night Daddy would let them out to eat and all he had to do was call them and they would go back in the cage.

Grandpa liked to give people nicknames. He called my father "Lit," short for "little man." The story goes that when Daddy and one of his cousins were babies, he kept crawling over to her and poking his finger in her eyes. Grandpa would say, "Little man, stop doing that." Daddy continued poking her eyes until Grandpa

Jesse Woodson James

aka

James Lafayette Courtney

★   ★   ★

PHOTO COMPARISONS

James L. Courtney and Jesse James . .

A family photograph of James L. Courtney.

. . . the same man.

famous photograph is accepted by
*es historians as being the real Jesse
*es. Experts have matched the Courtney
ly photo at left with this photo.

*Historians agree that this is a true photograph
of Jesse James as a teenager.*

The family portrait of James Courtney's mother (the author's great-great-grandmother) above was positively matched to the known photo of Zerelda James Samuel, mother of Jesse James, at bottom right, by Visic Corporation and the Austin Police Department's Forensic Multi-media Crime Lab. (In the pho the bottom right she is holding her eyeglasses.) Note the enlargement of the pattern of her dre right, which was proven identical to the dress worn in the Courtney family photo. White carna, have been said to be Zerelda's favorite flower; they are pictured on the purported grave of James. In several family photos, James Courtney's mother has a white carnation pinned to her d

. . . the same woman.

Historically accepted photo of Zerelda James Samuel.

James Courtney's mother, with arm missing . . .

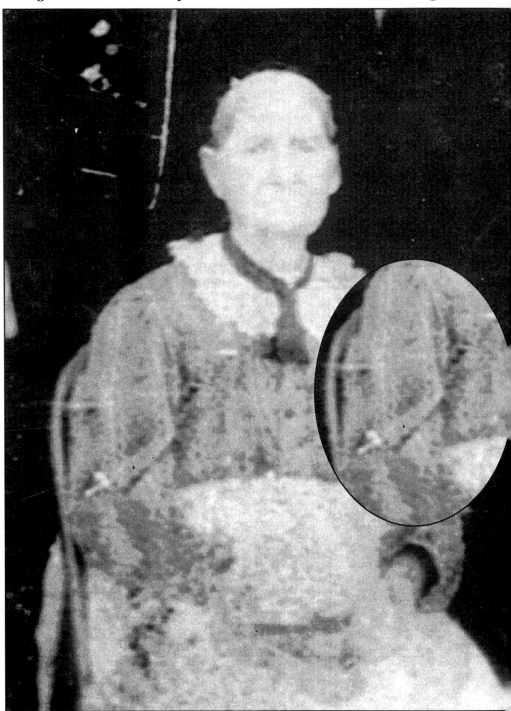

In this Courtney family photo, James Courtney's mother is clearly missing her right arm. Cl[o]se examination of the photo reveals a large pin in the middle of the right sleeve. When the auth[or] found this family photograph, she knew that her great-great-grandmother and Zerelda Sam[uel] were the same person.

Jesse James' mother, also missing an arm.

erelda James Samuel, the mother of Jesse, Frank, and Susan James, in a historically
ccepted photograph. What is left of her right arm is covered. It was shattered by the
inkerton bombing of her home and resulted in an amputation.

Dr. Reuben Samuel, in both the James and Courtney family collections.

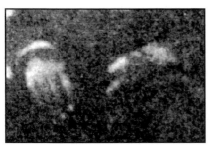

Dr. Reuben Samuel, stepfather of Jesse James, is pictured at right in a historically accepted photo. Below is the Courtney family photo of the man identified by Visionics Corporation and the Austin Police Department's Forensic Multi-media Crime Lab as the same person shown in the photo at right. Note that in both photos the top button of his shirt is buttoned—possibly the style of the day, and possibly an attempt to hide rope burns sustained when the Missouri militia pulled him up and down by the neck on a rope.

Enlargements show that the left ha in both photos apears to deformed. Dr. Samuel suffered cut the Pinkerton bombing that shatte Zerelda's arm. The author belie that those serious cuts were on left hand, and that because of injury another physician best Samuel performed the amputatior Zerelda's arm. (The author poir out the previously unrecogn deformity to staff at the James Fa Farm in Missouri.)

Same half-brother of Jesse!

...right is a photo of the boy identified by George ...rfel, photo authenticator for the James Farm, as ...hie Payton Samuel, half-brother of Jesse James. ...rfel said in the original of this photo the boy is stand- ...between two adults. In a Courtney family photo, above, ...boy identified by family members as a relative positively ...tches the boy in the portrait at right, according to Visionics ...rporation and the Austin Police Department's Forensic Multi-media Crime Lab.

Same boy — not Jesse's son, but his cousin's son?

Inset: *The historically accepted photo of Jesse Edwards James, claimed to be the son of Jesse James. The author believes this may actually be the son of Wood Hite.*

The boy in this Courtney family photo has been verified by experts to be the same boy as the or pictured in the inset portrait, historically known as Jesse James' son, Tim Howard aka Jes Edwards James. The people in this family portrait are unidentified, but the author believes th woman to be Jesse James' half-sister, Sarah (Sallie) Louisa Samuel Nickolson. The boy in bo photos was identified by Visionics Corporation and the Austin Police Department's Forens Multi-media Crime Lab to be the same person.

Jesse's half-sister

The photograph at right is historically identified as Sarah (Sallie) Louisa Samuel Nickolson, half-sister to Frank, Jesse, and Susan James. It is remark-bly similar to the portrait of the unidentified woman (above) from the Courtney family collection. Incidentally, James L. Courtney named one of his daughters Louisa.

Man in casket not Jesse James, but cousin Wood Hite?

*Death photograph of the man historically identified as Je~
James. The author believes the man to be Wood Hite, Jess
first cousin and a James Gang member. The man in the in~
photo was identified in Time-Life's* Gunfighters *as Jesse Jam~
however, George Warfel and Phillip Steele dispute this as being Jesse James in their book T*
Many Faces of Jesse James. *The author believes both of these assumed photos of Jesse James~
be Wood Hite, who was killed and buried under the identity of Jesse James. Members of the Jar~
Gang often declared themselves to be Jesse to confuse people about his identity.*

Jesse James, aka James Courtney, attending a Quantrill reunion of ex-Confederate guerrillas?

Grandpa (left) *standing next to a man who appears to be John Brown who rode with Quantrill. The man in the inset is identified as John Brown in Joanne Eakin and Donald Hale's* Branded As Rebels. *This photo was taken at a Quantrill reunion.*

Zee Mimms — Jesse's first cousin

A Courtney family photo at [...] believed to be Zee Mimm[...] Jesse's first cousin. History [...] reported that she was Jess[...] wife, but the author disagre[...] Experts have verified that [...] woman in this photo and the [...] below are the same person.

The historically accepted photograph of Zee Mimms, purported wife of Jesse James (and also his first cousin).

Jesse James

aka

James L. Courtney

★　　　★　　　★

FAMILY ALBUM

A Courtney family tintype of Jesse James, aka James Lafayette Courtney. The photograph is believed to have been made in Marlin, Texas, the county seat of Falls County where Courtney died at the age of ninety-six in 1943. The author owns this tintype.

James L. Courtney and his second wife, Edna Henry. The photo was taken around 1915, five years after his first wife, Mary Ellen, died.

James L. Courtney and his third wife, Ollie Nelson. Believed to be taken in the 1920s at his farm in Blevins, Texas.

Family photograph (tintype) o
James L. Courtney holding hi
daughter, Ida F. Courtney, th
paternal grandmother of th
author. Ida was born on April 5
1882, just three days after Jess
was purported shot dead by Bo
Ford.
—Photo courtesy of Bill Dorsett, th
    great-grandson of James Courtne

A family photograph of Ida Florence
Courtney, daughter of James and
Mary Ellen Courtney, around the
1920s.
    —Photo courtesy of Arthur Leon
    (Bubba) Campbell, great-grandson of
    James Courtney

James L. Courtney standing on the porch of his home in the late 1920s.

A family photograph of James L. Courtney, aka Jesse James, ca. 1900.

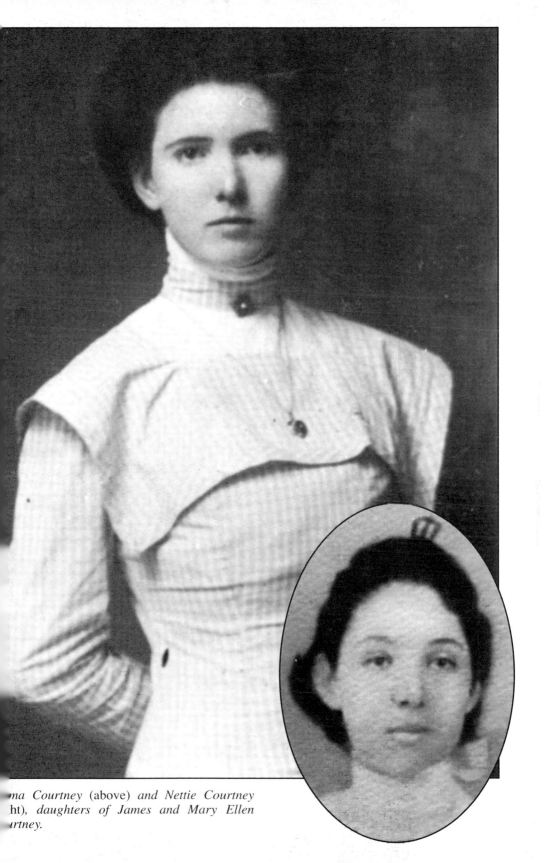

ma Courtney (above) *and Nettie Courtney* *(right), daughters of James and Mary Ellen* *Courtney.*

James L. Courtney, around the 1920s.
—Photo courtesy of Dorothy (Nell) Dorsett Hobbs Spurge
author's sister and great-granddaughter of James Court

anding in the very back from left to right: *Grandpa's son Byron Courtney and grandson Jesse llard Dorsett (in the black hat—the author's father.)*
anding in the front row left to right: *Lillie Courtney Yarborough (Grandpa's daughter), Joe rborough (Lillie's husband), Ida Courtney Dorsett (daughter of James L. Courtney), Mary Pearl la's daughter), and Mary's daughter.*
ated left to right: *One of Ida's great-granddaughters, James L. Courtney (Jesse James), and his rd wife, Ollie.*

nily photograph taken in the early 1930s. Left to right are (standing) *Lillie Courtney borough and Byron Courtney;* bottom row (sitting) *James L. Courtney, who died in 1943 at the of ninety-six, and Ida F. Courtney, his daughter and the author's grandmother.*

James L. Courtney seated in the center on the bottom row. His friends are seated on either side of him and their sons are standing behind. This photo is believed to have been taken in the 1920s.

Left: James L. Courtney in a family photo with his bee keeping equipment. He kept a large number of bee-hives over the years. He graduated from robbing banks to robbing bees!

The original house of James and Mary Ellen Courtney, which was demolished in 1940 to make way for a new home on the same site. Pictured at the back of the house with the kitchen to the right are (left to right) James L. Courtney, Byron Courtney, Mary Ellen (seated at left), and Willie Courtney (standing far right). Five of the people are unidentified. Ovals are enlargements of people in the photo.

The Courtney family in the late 1930s. Left to right are Ida Courtney, Lillie Courtney, James Courtney, Liza Busby, and Byron Courtney.

The author's parents, Dorothy Burt Dorsett and Jesse Willard Dorsett, taken June 25, 1963, their twenty-fifth wedding anniversary. Dorsett, who believed that his grandfather was Je James, dug for gold several times on the family farm that the family believes Courtney acquired from his days as Jesse James.

—Photo courtesy of Dorothy Burt Dorsett N

The last known photo of James L. Courtney with his family, believed taken in 1943, the year he [died]. Shown with him are Ida Courtney Dorsett Waechter (his daughter) and her second husband, [Paul] Waechter. The guns suggest that Courtney was still "a-huntin'" when he was ninety-six years [old]. He did not have to use the wheelchair at all times, just when his legs seemed to give out on [him].

This photograph was found in James L. Courtney's trunk after his death. Some of the people have been identified as family members from his home in Missouri. The author believes the boy on the far right to be Jesse's half-brother,

The author and her father on her wedding day—January 13, 1966. This photo was taken at Walnut Creek Baptist Church in Austin, Texas.

Joe B. Duke, husband of the author and father of Danny, Johnny, and Teresa.

The tombstone of James L. Courtney in the Blevins Cemetery, Blevins, Texas.

Robert L. (Bud) Dorsett and wife Judy. Bud is the grandson of James L. Courtney. Judy gave the author the treasure map drawn by James L. Courtney.

Howard William (Boy) Dorsett, the autho uncle and a grandson of James L. Courtney.

Jesse Wayne Dorsett, brother of the author and great-grandson of James L. Courtney.

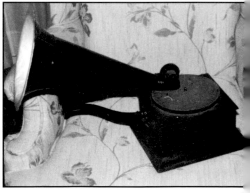

This is the old wind-up Victrola that led James L. Courtney's dismissal from the De Creek Baptist Church in Falls County, Texas

*ove: The author's daughter, Teresa Faye Duke, *tainly resembles her great-great-grandmother *ry Ellen Courtney.*

*ht: Mary Ellen Barron Courtney, the first wife *James Courtney and the author's great-grand-*ther, was the daughter of Capt. Thomas Hudson *rron, an early Texas Ranger who oversaw the *ding of Fort Fisher in Waco, Texas, now the *as Ranger Hall of Fame. Captain Barron is *ied in the First State Cemetery located adjacent *he old fort.*

—Family photo

A Courtney family photo of James L. Courtney (left) and his brother, who was curiously nam[ed] Fletcher Bagley, even though they were full-blood brothers. The author believes they were alia[ses] for Jesse and Frank James.

When the author's sons, Daniel (Danny) Joseph Duke and John (Johnny) Willard Duke, had [a] vintage-looking photo made to match that of their relatives above, just for fun, the photograp[her] jokingly said they really looked like Frank and Jesse James. One wonders if the photographe[r of] the photo above thought the same thing.

sternly said, "Lit, stop it!" The name stuck. He was called Lit from then on.

One day Grandpa Dorsett told his son Bud to take a fine stud horse they owned down to the river to water him. He told Bud to take care of that horse and not to let him get away.

Uncle Bud rode the horse to the river and never dismounted because he was afraid it would get away. They hadn't been at the river long when a wild stallion charged up to them. The two horses started fighting. They were rearing, kicking, and biting each other and the horse Uncle Bud was on killed the wild stallion. Uncle Bud couldn't have been over ten years old, but he stayed on that horse during the entire fight!

The Dorsetts were a rough, tough but good bunch of people. When the boys went skinny dipping they would whip each other with bull nettles to see who would be the sissy and jump in the water first. The Dorsett kids could swim like ducks.

Grandpa Courtney bought Ida a place where the Leon River and Cow House Creek meet. The Dorsett kids attended Tennessee Valley School and had to cross the Leon River by boat to get there.

Grandpa finally accepted Bill Dorsett into the family when he saw how happy his daughter Ida was. I'm awfully glad, because Grandpa Dorsett died at a young age (around forty). Ida, Bill, and the children had been to visit Grandpa and left late in the afternoon. They headed north toward Lorena and just before dark camped under a big oak tree near a creek (just off of what is now I-35). Grandma Dorsett cooked cornbread and cabbage for supper and then Grandpa Dorsett read aloud from the Bible just like he did every night. Several hours after he went to bed he had a nightmare and his family couldn't wake him up. Grandma Dorsett sent Daddy and Uncle Bud to get the doctor who lived miles away. The two boys, no older than ten and twelve, rode horseback in the darkness to get the doctor for their father. When they arrived back at camp their father was dead. The doctor said it was heart failure.

Relatives said they would never forget the covered wagon sitting in Grandpa's yard during the funeral. Some of them called Grandpa Dorsett Uncle Will, and said his children had never seen him in a suit and were fascinated at how handsome he looked.

Grandpa Courtney took care of all the funeral arrangements and buried my grandfather in Blevins Cemetery.

Byron Cambell Courtney was born in April 1884. He married Robbie Dacus. They started out on Grandpa's farm and had four children: Ida Mae, Naomi Evelyn, Byron, Jr., and Theresa Lavern.

Nettie Andruss Courtney was born on July 14, 1886. She married Hiram Shelton and they had five children: Bernice, Clarence, Vista, Hershel, and Eugenia. Her husband died when Eugenia was a baby and she lived on the farm. She cooked for Grandpa and did his laundry. When Grandpa remarried, Nettie moved to Oklahoma.

Emma Magdeline Courtney was born January 15, 1893, and married Lee Claypool. She was only a teenager when Grandma died in 1910. Emma and Grandpa were left alone. She was dating Emil Krause and they had marriage plans when she learned that she was pregnant with George Crawford's baby. The wedding was called off, but later on she married Mr. Claypool. Mr. Claypool had several sons and one daughter with his first wife and then adopted Emma's child, a girl named Jessie. They had two more girls, named Bernice and Virginia. When Emma died, Jessie went to stay the summer at Grandpa's. She was eighteen at the time. The two younger girls were sent to the Masonic Home in Fort Worth because by then Grandpa was too old to take care of them.

Not long after Grandpa married his third wife, Ollie, he paid cash for a 1919 model Ford car. Whenever he tried to drive it, he almost wrecked it, so he had other people take him where he needed to go. Grandpa was an expert when it came to riding horses, but being in his seventies I guess the transition was too much for him to make.

One day Grandpa asked my father and Uncle Bud to take him to Waco in his car. They were to arrive at Grandpa's house at a certain time but they were running late. When they pulled into Grandpa's driveway they were startled to see him taking the front fenders off his car. When they asked him what he was doing, he told them that if he was going to have to drive the thing he had to see which way he was going! He took care of his automobiles just like he did his horses. If his car started having any kind of trouble, no matter how minor, he bought a new one.

★   ★   ★

*When electricity became available to the
Blevins area, Grandpa would have no part
of it. He wouldn't allow the men from the
electric company to cross his property with
the power lines. He climbed onto the roof
of his house with his gun and yelled, "Aye
God, you Jayhawkers, get off my land!"
He never did get electricity in his home.
He just didn't trust it.*

★   ★   ★

Grandpa's son Byron had a chore that he had to do every single day (Byron lived with his father after his wife became mentally ill and was institutionalized). He had to count more than $50,000 in cash that Grandpa kept in a trunk in his house. The government had made everyone turn in their gold for currency, but Grandpa only turned in some of his gold and buried the rest. No one knows why it had to be counted every day.

One day shortly after Grandpa died, Byron went to dig for his father's buried treasure. He dug all day and found nothing. After all that hard digging he was very tired and decided to spend the night in Grandpa's house. He soon fell asleep but around midnight something woke him up. He looked around the room and was startled to see Grandpa standing in the doorway of the bedroom. He said Grandpa smiled and said, "You just missed it!"

Byron swore he was not dreaming and had never believed in ghosts until then.

It has been claimed that only some of the gold was found. Family members have passed on the story that a large portion of it may have been buried along the Leon River, which is now under Lake Belton.

People in the Blevins area reportedly didn't like Grandpa; he had a reputation of being a rich, grouchy, miserly old man. My father never saw that in him. He believed Grandpa grew tired of relatives using him. He said Grandpa would help anyone, but they

> ★   ★   ★
>
> *Grandpa told people that he "found" a lot of his money with a mineral rod. It has been said that Grandpa only used the mineral rod for show, tricking people into thinking that he "found" all that gold.*
>
> *One day a man came by trying to sell him a "new and improved" mineral rod; he said it was infallible. Grandpa just laughed and told the man he'd have to pass. What the man didn't know was that he was standing on top of some buried gold.*
>
> ★   ★   ★

only got one chance and if they blew that chance, that was it. If anyone ever lied to him, he was finished with them.

Grandpa was as good to people as they would let him be. When Ida's husband died, the depression of the 1930s made it next to impossible to support a family, especially for a widow with so many mouths to feed. Grandpa would load up the wagon with groceries and supplies and travel for many miles to deliver it to his daughter and grandchildren. My grandmother (Ida) and her children went to the cedar brakes to cut cedar to sell so they could make their own living. They did not want to depend on her father financially. I believe Grandpa really admired that quality in her because he left her two pieces of property in his will.

Some of my relatives referred to my grandmother and her children as "Cedar Choppers." Well, that's what they did, chop cedar. In my opinion, it's an honorable profession; they worked hard for their money.

Grandpa had very little formal education; he was self-educated. He was a born writer and recorded most of his life. He kept up with current events and politics. He subscribed to both Waco papers, the *Temple Daily Telegram,* and the *Congressional Record.*

★   ★   ★

*Two young boys from the Blevins area were
sneaking around Grandpa's barn, digging
for the treasure they'd heard so much about.
I guess you could call it beginner's luck
because they did find some money. They
took it home to their father, who promptly
returned it to Grandpa—fearing his wrath.
Grandpa told him no harm was done and
that he already knew about the missing loot
and who had taken it.*

★   ★   ★

Some of the magazines that he subscribed to were the *Dallas News, Semi-Weekly Farm News,* and *Farm and Ranch* magazine. His huge barn was said to be like a museum with newspapers from all over the country tied into bundles, like bales of hay and kept in storage there.

One night a couple of drunken relatives asked Grandpa if they could borrow some money from him. He refused them the loan. Later that night they burned his barn to the ground. I feel sick about the history that was lost that night due to stupidity.

My cousin said that many old friends came to sit on that back porch with its buckets of moss rose that Grandpa watered every morning, to talk of old times. The Bagleys, the O'Briens, and the Shooks were among the visitors. They were from elsewhere, not Blevins.

Grandpa went to a rodeo in Belton in the 1920s or 1930s. I wish I could have been there just to watch his expression because there was a man appearing there who claimed to be Jesse James! Grandpa bought two medallions that day, one picturing Jesse James and the other Buffalo Bill. Grandpa really enjoyed the show.

One of my cousin's best memories of Grandpa was the time he gave china cups for Christmas gifts. He liked pretty dishes. She said the thin, dainty cups lasted only briefly at her house, but she treasured the reality that Grandpa was a man of tenderness toward his children and the helpless. The cups were a symbol of something fine in his nature.

During Grandpa's years in Texas—which practically constituted a lifetime—he seemed to gain peace and satisfaction as a farmer and family man. The Jesse James of earlier times would lapse back only now and then.

Chapter 11

★ ★ ★

In His Own Words
(Grandpa's Diary)

*I*N 1871, GRANDPA AND a group of his friends left the Kansas City area and headed for Texas. As they were traveling through Indian territory they shot two buffaloes. A small party of Indians heard the shots and caught up with them. After seeing the buffalo meat and hides in the back of Grandpa's wagon, the Indians took the choicest meat and the hides, and then, using hand signals, pointed to Grandpa and the others and then to the far off horizon, letting them know to get off their land.

Grandpa always had a high regard for Native Americans and would travel long distances in his later years to visit their healers.

When the gang reached Decatur, Texas, Grandpa bought a book for fifty cents in which to record daily occurrences. It is believed that he kept a diary most of his life, but I have only located his diaries for the years 1871, 1872, 1874, and 1876.

He wrote of weddings, births, deaths, and everyday life in nineteenth-century Texas. It may be a surprise to find out that a man from that era, and especially an outlaw, helped his wife take care of their children and even helped wash clothes. In those days that was considered women's work and was demeaning for men.

The following entries were transcribed from Grandpa's original diaries just as he wrote them.

Fiddler's Green

Halfway down the trail to hell
In a shady meadow green,
Are the souls of all dead troopers camped
Near a good old-time canteen
And this eternal resting place
Is known as Fiddler's Green.

Marching past, straight through to hell,
The infantry are seen,
Accompanied by the Engineers,
Artillery and Marine,
For none but the shades of Cavalrymen
Dismount at Fiddler's Green.

Though some go curving down the trail
To seek a warmer scene,
No trooper ever gets to Hell
Ere he emptied his canteen,
And so rides back to drink again
With friends at Fiddler's Green.

And so when man and horse go down
Beneath a saber keen,
Or in a roaring charge or fierce melee
You stop a bullet clean,
And the hostiles come to get your scalp,
Just empty your canteen,
And put your pistol to your head
And go to Fiddler's Green.

1871

June 1871
28 Wensday   for book 50
                                         for wagon grease 25

29 Thirsday morning
          for milk   25
at Decatur in camp back of the tin shop and remained there all
day and in the evening went ahunting with H Pratt and Edward
Sunderland and the tavern keep, and I killed a deer.

30 Friday morning in camp back of the tin shop and rized up for
to start south
          for corn ½ lb   75
          for caps for gun   75
I then traveled south just about 12 mile from Decatur we crossed
Denton Creck and then traveled down on the East side of the
creek and camped at a mans house by the name of Burnett

Spent during the month of June the sum of $26^{30}

July 1871
1 Saturday morning in camp at Burnetts on Denton Creek and
then started for Elizabeth town and crossed Denton 2 mile from
camp and then traveled 4 miles and crossed [illeg.] creek and
traveled on to Elizabeth and camped on the creek south of town
the distance we traveled in the fore noon was 10 miles
          for sweet milk   15
          for corn 1 bus   1.20

2 Sunday morning in camp at Elizabeth in camp south creek of
the town i remained there all day

3 Monday morning in camp at Elizabeth town and started for
Fort Worth and traveled 10 mile and camped on the big focel and
then traveled into town

for eggs	15
for melon	25
for shugar	50
for soda	10
for horse shewing	100

and then went down ~~the river and camped on the Trinity river sent Frank to~~ clearfork and camped and at nite moved 2 mile in the country the distance was 20 m

4 Tusday morning in camp 2 mile west of Fort Worth and then rized up and went into town and stade there untill noon and then start to the country with and old (n   )

for 6 bars of led   45

left Henry Pratt, Edward Sunderland, Albert Crosgrove & George Millind at Fort Worth on the fourth of July and I went out 4 mile west of town and stade the rest of the day and the nite and eat 3 meals

for lodging on the fourth of July   50

5 Wensday morning started from four miles west of Fort Worth and traveled about 12 mile and stopped for noon at a mans by the named of Gililung on Mustand Creek in Tarant Co and I crossed Marys creek dutch branch before I camp for noon and in the evening I traveled 8 mile and camped at the last house at the edge of the timber as I was coming to Stevenvill about 4 mile below Robinsons old mill

for eggs i doz	15
for buter 1 lb	15

6 Thirsday traveled 12 mile before noon and camped at noon on the west side of the Brazess R. and i crossed 2 creeks before i crossed the river but i don't no the name of them

for corn 1 bushel   1^{00}

bought this corn on the west side of the Brasess R. on the edge of the little log town of and old lady at the last house at the west end of town and after noon passed through Grandbery and then went to Powels and camped for the night on the branch below the house and remained there all nite the distance that i traveled today is 20 m

7 Friday morning in camp at Powels and rized up to move on and Old Gentleman went with me to Stevensvill we traveled about 5 mile and crossed a branch and then went about 11 mile

and crossed a creek by the name of Stephens or Polaxy and then went on to Polaxy creek and camped for noon and the old gent went to the house for diner He went to Hill for diner and i rized up and we drove into town that is Stephenville and then i went about 1 mile south of town and camped for the nite

8 Saturday morning in camp 1 mile south of town at a mans by the name of C Penny and then went into town and stade some time and returned to camp and found things all rite & moved camp back on the east side of town on the east side of the creek and remained there the rest of the day and nite

9 Sunday morning in camp east of town & went to church and then returned to camp & then went to Mr Painters for diner
    for 1 sack of salt   15
& after noon went into town & stade there untill nearly nite & then returned to camp and stade there the rest of the evening & the nite

10 Monday morning in camp east of town and remained there all day that is the town stade there i was in town nearly all the time
    for beaf liver   5

11 Tusday morning in camp east of town and stade there untill noon and i let W.C. Painter have my horse to rid in the fore noon & he kept him all day
    for one pan of milk   10

12 Wensday morning in camp east of town and stad there all day
    for washing 4 shirts   40
    to wite ones & 2 colored ones
    for sulpher   10

13 Thirsday morning in camp East of town and remained there all day & let the sherif have one of my pistols

14 Friday morning in camp East of Stephenvill & lost aplaying tenpins 5^{25}

15 Saturday morning in camp East of Stephenvill and remained there all day Exchanged 20 dolars in curincy
    for 18 in spishia   exchange 2^{00}
    for honey   70

for shugar	30

16 Sunday morning in camp east of Stephenvill and remained there all day

for coal oil	5
for ink	10
for milk	10

17 Monday morning in camp East of Stephenvill and remained there all day

for soape	25

18 Tusday morning started from Stephenvill for Meridian

for meat	35
for curacomb	25

and traveled 30 m and camped on the Bosque and I chilled in the nite

19 Wensday morning in camp at the Bosque and started on for Medidian and there was a man with me by the name of Morgain passed through Meridian and the felow left me he pade me 1 dolar for riding and then i went 5 mile and camped for noon & then hitched up and went into *Clifton* and there camped for the nite

for egg 1 doz	15

20 Thirsday morning in camp at *Clifton* I starts for Waco

for peaches	25
for water melon	10

the distance that i traveled to day was 20 mile and camped at the first house after crossing the big prarie

21 Friday morning in camp 12 mile from Waco and hitched up and traveled into town against 11 oclock and mailed to leters one to unkle and the other home and then drove 3 mile & camped for the nite

for 15 lb flour	1^{00}
for baking bread	25

22 Saturday morning in camp 3 miles west of Waco & hitched up and traveled 10 mile to H. Crawfields and camped for the nite the distance is 12 miles

23 Sunday morning in camp at H. Cranfields and remained there all day

24 Monday morning in camp at H. Cranfields & hitched up & went to Thomas Barrons and camped for the nite the distance traveled was 20 mile
    stoped

25 Tusday morning in camp at Barrons
for corn 1 bushel in yers & remained there all day   1^{00}

26 Wensday morning in camp at Barrons and remained there all day
    for one botle of Honey   25

27 Thirsday morning in camp at Barrons and remained there all day and in the evening went a hunting with the Schoolmaster but did not see anything

28 Friday morning in camp at Barrons and remained there all day
    For washing to shirts   25
    for boots   5.^{00}
    for coffee   50
    for shugar   50

29 Saturday morning in camp at Barrons and rized up for meeting
    for melon   25

30 Sunday morning at [illeg.] went to meeting with Bud and David and returned at dark on Sunday evening

31 Monday morning went to work amaking a hay farming till noon and after noon halled hay

    Spent during the month of July the sum of $25.30
    $121.00 spent up to July 31 from the time i left home

August 1871
1 Tusday morning in camp on the praries and halled 2 loads of hay

2 Wensday halled hay all day halled 2 loads

3 Thirsday halled hay to Lords and quit at 8 oclock untill evening

4 Friday morning at Barons and went to get my horses shod
    for shewing   1^{50}
and returned at dark

5 Saturday morning at Mr. Barrons and went ahunting with Mr.
Crow and Baron in the fore noon and after noon went to meeting with Bud Baron and the boys and stade all nite at Travs
    for melon   25

6 Sunday morning at Mr Trav Barrons with Bud and Huse and
the girls and went to meeting at 11 oclock & and the boys& the
rest of them went in the hack with david
    for melon   20

7 Monday morning at Barons and remained there all day &
halled a load of wood with david and Bud

8 Tusday at Mr Barrons and remained there all day and i hepe
the girls cut peaches to day

9 Wensday morning at Mr Barrons and remained there all day

10 Thirsday morning at Mr. Barrons and remained there all day

11 Friday morning at Mr Barrons & Travis & his wife were there
and a man by the name of Singleton

12 Saturday morning at Mr Barrons and went ahunting with
Crow Bud Singleton & Barron & in the evening went to trav
Barrons & worked to young horses

13 Sunday morning at Mr Trav Barrons and went to meeting
with Bud Singleton and Mr Travis Barron & returned at nite

14 Monday morning at Mr Barrons & stacked hay till 9 oclock
and then returned to the house we worked about 2 hours

15 Tusday morning at Barrons & gathered corn untill noon &
halled corn after noon with my wagon & harness and i drove the
young horses

16 Wensday at Barrons and went ahunting with david and after noon with David and Singleton and Bud Barron

17 Thirsday morning at Mr Barrons and helped Bud shell 3 bushels of corn for to go to mill

18 Friday morning at Mr Barrons and stade at the house all day and do nothing untill noon and the same after noon

19 Saturday morning at Mr Barrons and remained there all day & I killed a deer in the morning and David killed one in the evening

20 Sunday morning . . . . & Bud started for Waco and i remained at the house all day & Mrs Barron baked pie

21 Monday morning at Mr Barrons & halled corn with David halled in my wagon we halled all day & we halled 5 loads from a man by the name of Right

22 Tusday morning at Mr Barrons and me & David halled corn all day we halled 4 loads 1 from Rites and 3 from Barrons Baby I worked me and my wagon

23 Wensday morning at Mr Barrons and me and David toped the hay stack and then halled corn till noon in the litle field at the house & in the evening halled corn halled 2 loads me Jack & Bud & we used my wagon

24 Thirsday morning at Mr Bs and halled corn all day halled one load to Estep and 2 loads home used my wagon

25 Friday morning at Mr Bs and it is raining & we done nothing all day only fix the chimney

26 Saturday morning at Mr Bs & went and halled 1 load of corn from Esteps and returned at 10 oclock and then done nothing the rest of the day

27 Sunday morning at mr b and remained there all day
    for riting paper   15
    sulpher   15

28 Monday morning at Mr B and remained there all day and do nothing stade at the house all day

29 Tusday morning at Mr B & gethered corn until 11 oclock with Jack & David I was sick after noon

30 Wensday morning at B and gathered corn all day me & David & Jack and we worked my wagon we halled 1 load from Esteps and from the litle field before noon and 4 loads after noon we used my wagon

Got Jack Townly to wash my quilts & 3 shirts [illeg.]

The amount that I spent during the month $7.25 and I used a 75 yeers of corn and one barrel of corn up to the 31 of August

September 1871
1 Friday morning at Mr Barrons & me and David Jack & Mr Crow halled a load of wood & then we shelled 3 bushcls of corn against noon we used my wagon & Jack halled a load in my wagon & do nothing after noon stade at the house all the evening only a litle while I went to Jack's and the girls was there to

2 Saturday morning at mr B & made brush fence till noon & the same after noon I worked with Jack Tounly

3 Sunday morning at Mr B & rote three leters one to Wm McKinsls & Joe S & Uncle Jacob Hawn & remained at Mr Barrons all day

4 Monday morning at Mr B & made brush fence untill noon with Jack & pade Crow for a gun
    for gun 10^{00}

5 Tusday morning at Mr B & shelled corn for David we gathered 5 loads and we used my wagon

6 Wensday morning at Mr Barrons & went to gathern corn for David Huse we gathered 2 loads before noon & 3 loads after noon and used my wagon

7 Thirsday morning at Mr B and gathered corn for david we gathered 3 loads in the fore noon and the captain came home &

brought 1½ yard of cloth to finish my pants we used my wagon & we finished gathering corn by noon and Mrs Barron made me a pair of pants the price is not know as yet

    1½ yards of cloth cost 75 cts per yard $1^{12½}$

8 Friday morning at Mr B & me and Jack made brush fence until noon and after noon do nothing & I went ahunting in the evening but didn't see anything

9 Saturday morning at B & reseived $1.00 dolar by cash and I went to Mastervill & bought 10 postage stamps   30

    for c18dy   50

and returned at 1 oclock and stade at the house the rest of the day

10 Sunday morning at Mr B & went to meeting me Jack his wife Ellen Serena & a lady from Waco and we returned at 3 oclock and remained there all day and I went and stade all nite with Jack

11 Monday morning at Mr B & me & David went to Camp creek which was 12 mile & returned at 2 oclock we went there for the purpose of looking for water so that we could cut hay but found none & in the evening helped Townley bild his chimney he was to pay me 50 cts or a half of a dy work

12 Tusday morning at Mr Barrons & Mr B and Eanus started for Waco in the buggy and Mr B returned at dark me & Jack went ahunting & I killed a turkey & Mr Barron brought my gun when he came this 12 of September

13 Wensday morning at Mr B & remained there all day & at nite went to Elisons for a dance & danced all nite & returned here at daylight & Miss B made me [illeg.]

14 Thirsday morning at Mr B & went with him to look for hay to cut & returned before noon and the rest of the day do nothing untill nite and then went ahunting and it rained & i got wet as a rat & I got a part of a flask of powder of the old mans & some shot

15 Friday morning at Mr B & do nothing before noon & after noon shell 3 bushels of corn and Jack and I went ahunting

16 Saturday morning at Mr B & do nothing before noon & Jack halled some poles for to build a hay pen with my wagon & after noon do nothing

17 Sunday morning at Mr B & remained there all day & David went to Mastervill & the revenew season called for the nite

18 Monday morning at Mr B & helped Jack make a hay pen before noon & after noon do nothing only me & Jack went to Babys ahunting and returned at nite

19 Tusday morning at Mr Barrons & remained there all day and was grunting & taken a dose of P afternoon & the captain went to Mastervill in the morning & returned at nite

20 Wensday morning at Mr B & halled 1 load of wood by myself and remained there the rest of the day and in the evening traided my wagon horses & harness to a man by the name of Linza I traided them for 36 heads of cows and calfs between the age of 3 & 5 years old he taken the things off with him the same evening

21 Thirsday morning at B & remained there all day & do nothing

22 Friday morning at Mr B and repared the pen before noon and caught up a horse & in the evening do nothing & stayed at the house

23 Saturday morning at Mr Barons and remianed there all day and do nothing

24 Sunday morning at Mr Barrons and me and David went to Mastervill and I rode the sorel and returned at 2 oclock and Mr Bures and his wife was there and I remained there the rest of the day and do nothing

25 Monday morning at Mr Barrons and do nothing in the fore noon and in the after noon got some poles for to make a gate to the pen and after noon boared the holes through the post

26 Tusday morning at Mr Barrons and made a gate for the pen

and then do nothing before noon and after noon went to Linzes
and returned at nite

27 Wensday morning at Mr Barrons and remained there all day
and do nothing settled with Miss Townly for washing one ½
month
     pade cash 1^{50} on the 27 of September   1^{50}

28 Thirsday morning at Mr Barrons & he started for Waco but
didn't go he returned in the evening and Travas Barron came
with him and I remained at the house all day and do nothing

29 Friday morning at Mr Barrons and remained there untill noon
& after noon went with the old gent to look for his horses and
returned at nite

30 Saturday morning at Mr Barrons and remained there all day
and do nothing only mark the pigs in the fore noon and after
noon went ahunting

Spent during the month of September the sum of $2.30

October 1871
1 Sunday morning at Mr Barrons and remained there all day and
Travis went to Mastervill in the evening

2 Monday morning at Mr Barrons and it is raining & it rained
all nite & i remained at the house till noon and after noon went
ahunting and returned at nite didnt kill anything

3 Tusday morning at Mr Barrons and stade at the house untill
noon & after noon went to Linzes and returned at nite and do
nothing all day

4 Wensday morning at Mr Barrons & Mr Barron started for
Waco and i remained at the house all day and do nothing Mr
Elison & Mr Morison was hear and David Hugh fixed his fince

5 Thirsday morning at Mr Barrons and remained there all day
and do nothing only at nite went ahunting and returned at day

6 Friday morning at Mr Barrons and me and Mr Huse went to
Mr Linzys and returned at noon and then went to look for cows
and found one

7 Saturday morning at Mr Barrons and me and David Huse went to look for cattle and found none and returned at 2 oclock and i remained at the house the rest of the day and do nothing and the Old Man returned at nite and Bud came with him

8 Sunday morning at Mr Barrons & remained at the house all day and Trav came and Shelton came at nite and he seemed if he was in grate trouble

9 Monday morning at Mr Barrons and me and Bud halled rails till noon and after noon fixed the pen and ran a partition in the pen to hold the calfs and Shelton & Travis & Huse was there

10 Tusday morning at Mr Barrons & me and Bud started to hunt for cattle went to Tompsons and then went on and overtaken cox and camped at Whits at the Oald H C [illeg.] place
Bud 1

11 Wensday morning at Whits place and started to hunt for cattle with 2 coxes & Linzes & rite & to more men came to us as we were starting off and we camped at Mr Sanfords & stade all nite and Bud & i stade with them and helped to gather catle
Bud 2

12 Thirsday morning started from Sanfords and went home that day & i reseived 6 cows and calfs and B cox helped to drive them home
Bud 3

13 Friday morning at Mr Barrons & remained at the house all day and do nothing only killed a beaf a black one

14 Saturday morning at Mr B and me and Bud went to Miss Bakers and returned at noon and it rained all day

15 Sunday morning at Mr Barrons and remained at the house all day and Shelton returned home to his family

16 Monday morning at Mr Barrons and me and Bud went to Elam to the Shith Shop and brought one of the old mans cows and returned at nite & got one of Linzes cows
Bud 4

17 Tusday morning at Mr Barrons & me & Bud & T Barron
went and looked for cows and found one and returned at nite
                    Bud 5

18 Wensday morning at Mr B & me and Dow halled aload of
wood in the fore noon & in the evening me & Bud halled 1 load

19 Thirsday morning at B & me and Bud went to the house
raysing to Mr Morises and returned at nite & the 46d 718 g3ve
h3s c4s28t f49 73 t4 hlve 26628 & Bud & Davy & Travis went
to the party
[Code translated: "Old man give his consent for me to have
Ellen"]

20 Friday morning at Mr Barrons & me Bud & Travis went to
Pan Creek to look for cows & found 1 returned at 2 oclock &
Bud went to the shop for the branding irons
      for Branding iron 1^{00}

B6

21 Saturday morning at Mr Barrons and remained there all day
& helped davy shell corn in the fore noon and in the evening do
nothing & stade at the house

22 Sunday morning at Mr Barrons and remained at the house all
day & Shelton and his wife was here & Miss Rite and Trave
Barron was here & Bud went to morisses and returned at dark

23 Monday morning at mr Barrons and stade at the house untill
noon and then went out to where rabeleses was gathering catle
and returned at nite

24 Tusday morning at Mr Barrons and started a cow hunting
with Rabeleses and went down to Tompsons and then turned for
home me & Bud & the Old Gentleman returned from Waco &
brought me a coat which cost the sum
      for a coat 5^{25}

25 Wensday morning at Mr Barrons and helped Reese to hall
logs for to bild a crib for to put his cow in in the fore noon & in
the after noon helped him to put up the crib and put his cow in
it & he started for home

26 Thirsday morning at Mr Barrons & remained there all day & do nothing & in the evening Bud went off

27 Friday morning at Mr Barrons & start for Marlin & reached Marlin a 2 oclock

for fery	25
for recording branch	75
for mariage lisens	150
for hat pants Boots neckty & hickry shirtin	15.50
for fery	25

and then came out to Parson Taylors and stade all nite

28 Saturday morning at Mr Taylors and started for home & reached home at noon & Mr Coal was there & the Old Gentleman was gone to Mastervill & i remained at the house the rest of the day & calwell pened here in the evening and Branded

29 Sunday morning at Mr Barrons & remained there all day & Shelton was there & a man by the name of Cuningham & Trav Barron

30 Monday morning at Mr Barrons and went a cow hunting with calwell and Bud went & we found 2 cows & Blackwell & his sisters was here

31 Tusday morning at Mr Barrons & (Dow & his sisters was there & Calwell & his cowhunters was here & Cuningham & in the evening i was married by Parson Taylor & he charged me for his service

for parsonage   5^{00}

Pade Bud by Cuningham on the first of November by cash of Mr Barron of the 1 of November 1.00 for to pay Parson Taylor
Spent during October the sum of $30=50

November 1871
1 Wensday morning at Mr Baron & in the fore noon do nothing & in the evening went a cow hunting with Bud Trav & Cuningham & returned at nite with one [illeg.] cow & 1 [illeg.] cow & marked 4 for D Mixen

2 Thirsday morning at Mr Barrons & me & Bud went down on elam to Calwell & then returned home at noon & after noon Bud went to mixens & i remained at the house the rest of the day and do nothing

★ ★ ★

*Some may question why dates and places in
Grandpa's diary don't correspond with the dates
given for some of the robberies attributed to the
James Gang. The best answer I have to that
question came from Cole Younger himself, in his
autobiography,* The Story of Cole Younger. *He took
a solemn oath that he never robbed a bank in
Missouri, and also denies the following bank and
train robberies:*

1. *March 20, 1868—Russelville, Kentucky*
2. *June 3, 1871—Obocock Bros. Bank, Corydon,
   Iowa*
3. *April 29, 1872—Columbia, Kentucky*
4. *September 26, 1872—Kansas City Fair robbery*
5. *July 21, 1873—Iowa train robbery*

*Though Cole Younger denies having taken part in
those robberies, historical accounts state otherwise.
Since I don't have much confidence in historical
accounts concerning the James Gang, it's hard to say
who was telling the truth. Therefore, the fact that the
dates in Grandpa's diary say he was in one place
when historical accounts report that Jesse was elsewhere may indicate that either the reports are wrong or
Grandpa may have used his diary as an alibi in case
he was ever captured. He was always thinking ahead.*

★ ★ ★

3 Friday morning at Mr B and remained there untill noon & then
started a cow hunting with Bud Dave Mixon and a boy and
camped on north elam

4 Saturday morning in camp on north elam and hunted down
the creek all day and found 11 cows and then went across [illeg.]
Pan Creek and pened for the nite at Mrs Hunt & Williams hands
was there

5 Sunday morning at Miss Hunts and hunted cows all day and camped at Davises

6 Monday morning at Davises and crossed Pan Creek & loss four cows & then reached into Pauls prairie and then started for home and reached home at nite Alisons was with us 3½ days

7 Tusday morning at Mr Barrons & remained there all day and do nothing & it rained till noon & in the after noon we killed a beaf Bud Davy & myself

8 Wensday morning at Mr Barrons and do nothing only went ahunting in the fore noon with Davy & in the evening went by self and didn't see any thing

9 Thirsday morning at Mr Barrons & remained there at the house all day & do nothing only clean out the spring

10 Friday morning at Mr Barrons and went to Linzys and returned at 2 oclock & Old Man Hater was there & Bud & Davy went to morisses to help him rays a smoke house & then went to Alisons to a party & there was to other men here & i received a leter from Jacob Haun

11 Saturday morning at Mr Barrons & remained at the house all day & do nothing

12 Sunday morning at Mr Barrons & i rote a leter to Unkle Jacob Haun & remained at the house all day

13 Monday morning at Mr Barrons and i remained at the house all day and do nothing

14 Tusday morning at Mr Barrons & i went down to Linzys & he came and looked at the cows and taken out 3 and told Mr Baron to see the rest branded [illeg.] was 23 cows and calfs and Bud & Davy Huse helped me Brand then we comenced after noon we branded 4 cows before noon

15 Wensday morning at Mr Barrons and me & Bud & Davy branded 22 calfs Davy helped ½ day & in the evening do nothing & Bud went to D. Mixens

16 Thirsday morning at Mr Barrons & started a cow hunting with Bud & Davy Mixen & camped at Cask Pestry & branded 5 calfs for Mixen and remained at his pen all nite

17 Friday morning at Mr Casks & hunted cows all day & branded 2 calfs for me one of the (ard) & one H cows & calf the cow wasnt branded & it rained nearly all nite

18 Saturday morning at Betz & went to Mastervill & then home & remained there & trav Barron was there

19 Sunday morning at Mr Barrons & me & Ellen went to Mr Grigses and stade all day and returned at nite

20 Monday morning at Mr Barrons & me Davy & Bud killed a beaf in the fore noon & in the after noon we worked Buten & chuck to the school house & Buck & T. Baren was here he came here on the 18 of this month & reese moved down his wife and two boys

21 Tusday morning at Mr Barrons & remained there all day and do nothing

22 Wensday morning at Mr Barrons & remained there all day and do nothing & Trav & Paw started to Waco

23 Thirsday morning at Mr Barrons & remained at the house all aday and do nothing & David Vestell came there in the evening

24 Friday morning at Mr B and remained there all day and do nothing

25 Saturday morning at Mr Barrons & Mr Campbell came there & Bud started to hunt the horses and David Vestel was there and remained there all day & Ellen was sick

26 Sunday morning at Mr Barrons & me and D. Huse went a pecanHunting and returned at 8 oclock and Bud & Serena started to Mis Bakers for the pecan hunting

27 Monday m at M Barrons and remained at the house untill noon and then after noon halled 1 load of wood

28 Tusday morning at Mr B and went a hunting & killed 1 w

362c1t and Boby was there in the afternoon & i done nothing all day

29 Wensday morning at Mr Barrons and remained at the house all day and do nothing only hall 1 load of wood

30 Thirsday morning at Mr Barrons and it sleeted all day and we remained at the house and do nothing

Spent during the month of November the sum 0^{00}

December 1871
1 Friday morning at Mr Barron and helped to kill 4 hogs in the after noon me & Bud & Davy and in the fore noon me & Davy halled a load of wood

2 Saturday morning at Mr Barrons and remained there all day & helped davy hall a load of wood

3 Sunday morning at Mr Barrons and remained there all day and Shelton and his wife was there

4 Monday morning at Mr B's and remained there all day and do nothing only take down the chimney & camell & Trav B was there

5 Tusday morning at Mr Barron and remained there all day and do nothing and Bud started to Marlin with Grigs and camell left

6 Wensday m at Mr Barrons and helped Bud shell 4 bushel of corn in the fore noon & Bud returned from Marlin in the morning

7 Thirsday morning at Mr Barron and halled 3 loads of poals for to fit the fence and the rest of the day do nothing and stade at the house

8 Friday morning at Mr Barrons and helped dow hall a load of wood in the fore noon and in the after noon do nothing

9 Saturday morning at M Barrons and went a hunting and killed a fon and the old Gentleman started for Waco and Trav went to Mastervill

10 Sunday morning at Mr Barron & me & Ellen & Lue went to Sheltons and returned at Dark

11 Monday m at Mr Barrons and i went ahunting all day and killed 1 turkey

12 Tusday m at Mr Barrons & made fence all day & Trav & Paw & John Powers returned from Waco and all drunk

13 Wensday morning at Mr Barrons and J Powers starts for home and Bud & Trav went with him home and i went ahunting in the evening & killed a venson

14 Thirsday morning at Mr Barrons & remained there all day & do nothing

15 Friday morning at Mr Barrons & killed hogs untill noon and in the after noon do nothing

16 Saturday morning at Mr Barrons and went ahunting in the fore noon and killed a deer & in the afternoon went to look for a beaf with Bud & Mr Rese & didn't see anything and Dow Blackwell was here when i got to the house & the Old Man and Davy went off & Paw did not return

17 Sunday m at Mr Barrons & remained there all day & Dow Blackwell was here and Rese & his family was there

18 Monday morning at Mr Barrons & me & Trav & Bud went to shelling corn for the grist mill and we shelled corn untill noon & in the after noon we done nothing and Bud rized the wagon for to start to Waco

19 Tusday morning at Mr Barrons & Bud & Trav started for Waco & i remained at the house all day and do nothing & Elisson was here

20 Wensday morning at Mr Barrons and me Rese Davy & Mr Grigs went ahunting and Rese killed a deer and returned at dark

21 Thirsday morning at Mr Barrons and me & Davy halled wood all day & in the evening Bud & Trav returned from Waco & Miley came with them &

22 Friday morning at Mr Barrons & Miley was there & Travis & me & went to look for a beaf and returned at dark

23 Saturday morning at Mr Barrons and do nothing in the fore noon & in the after noon went to look for a beaf with Mr Rese & his boys & returned at dark

24 Sunday morning at Mr Barrons and Miley & Travis & Sal & his old man was there & Mr Rese & all his family and i remained at the house all day and do nothing

25 Monday morning at Mr Barrons Miley Travis Reses & Sal and his old man was there and Travis Bud Davy & Sals man went to Alisons to [illeg.] a house & returned at noon

26 Tusday morning at Mr Barrons & me & Ellen went home with Miley anad Davy went with us & then returned home & me & Ellen remained at Miles

27 Wensday morning at Thads & helped him to take out his dishes & remained at Thads all day

29 Friday morning at T Mixens & remained there all day
        For Boots   4^{50}

30 Saturday morning at T Mixens and remained there all day and do nothing & Travis & Davy came there in the evening and stade there all day & do nothing

31 Sunday morning at T Mixen & remained there until noon & in the after noon went home with Davy & Sal & her man was there and Reid and they remained there

Spend During the month of December the Sum of $4^{50}

Spent During the year 1871 the sum of $165

1872

January 1872
1 Monday morning at Mr Barrons & remained there all day & do nothing for i was sick all day & Bud & Eli started for Waco

2 Tusday morning at Mr Barrons and cut poles all day cut 110 and quit before nite

3 Wensday morning at Mr Barrons & halled poles till noon and in the after noon bilt fence & miss read & H. Rite was there & Bud & Eli returned from Waco

4 Thirsday morning at Mr Barrons & fixed fence all day untill about 3 ocl and then went ahunting

5 Friday morning at Mr Barrons and set out his cherry trees in the morning and then bilt fence till noon & in the after noon do nothing

6 Saturday morning at Mr B & remained at the house and do nothing

7 Sunday morning at Mr B & illen went to rites with Sal & Bill Reid returned at home at nite and Mr Straw was there

8 Monday morning at Mr B & bilt fence all day & Mr Straw was there & Sals man started for the railroad & Mr Coal stade all nite

9 Tusday morning at Mr Barrons & bilt fence & hanged meat untill noon & in the after noon I done nothing

10 Wensday morning at Mr B and was sick all day and remained at the house all day and was in bed nearly all the time

11 Thirsday morning at Mr B & remained at the house all day and was sick

12 Friday morning at Mr Barrons and remained there all day and do nothing only fix the fence at the stack & Sals man returned in the evening from the railroad

13 Saturday morning at Mr Barrons & went ahunting and Paw Bud & Eli went to help Mr Read move his house & Davy & William went after Sal to Mastervill and i returned at noon

14 Sunday morning at Mr Bs & went ahunting and killed to turkey and returned at noon & D Vestal & Malisa was there

15 Monday morning at Bs & went ahunting & killed a deer & in the evening went to look for cows & returned at nite

16 Tusday morning at Bs and went to look for cows & returned at noon and in the after noon branded 2 apese and 3 for Paw & returned home at noon & in the after noon i branded 2 cows & 2 calfs 1 cow branded H &   1 calf was branded & i branded 5 yearling

17 Wensday morning at Mr Bs and went to Pan Creek and pened at Baby and branded 2 apese and 3 for paw & returned home at noon & in the after noon went and got 4 and branded 1 for me

18 Thirsday morning at Bs & it rained all day & i done nothing

19 Friday morning at Bs & helped hall 3 loads of wood & 1 load of hay & Bety came to Travis and made friends with him

20 Saturday morning at Mr Bs & cow hunted all day with Bud Eli Rese & his boy and got calfs for 72 & 92s2 G4t 8382 [Translated: "Me & Rese Got nine"]

21 Sunday morning at Barrons & remained there all day I Mr & Mrs Reed left here this morning & Eli & Sal they went to Rites

22 Monday morning at Mr Bs & went to the timber for to make ax [illeg.] & after noon went to look for a wolf and returned at nite & i received of T. H. Barron the sum of 75 for to get stamps & [illeg.]

23 Tusday morning at Mr B and hanged meat & bilt a [illeg.] till noon & Bud & William returned from Marlin at noon & do nothing in the after noon

24 Wensday morning at Barrons & went to the timber with William and we cut 2 loads of wood & then returned to the house and it snowed all day and then after noon do nothing & Read & his wife came here in the morning & Miley came down

25 Thirsday morning at Barrons Dow Miley Read & his wife was here & in the evening Parson Taylor came & married William & Serena & Bud & Poca and i remained at the house all day & done nothing only bild fires for the rest to quarrel over

26 Friday morning at Paws & me & Eli halled wood & William Serena went home & the Parson to & in the after noon i fixed the stove

27 Saturday morning at Barrons and went ahunting & killed a turkey & returned at noon and in the afternoon do nothing

28 Sunday morning at Barrons & remained there all day & rote 2 leters one to Rat & the other to Cosin Theodore & miley was here

29 Monday morning at Barrons & helped Davy & Eli hall wood we halled all day & in the evening halled a load of hay

30 Tusday morning at Barrons & went ahunting & returned at noon and in the after noon done nothing

31 Wensday morning at Barrons & cut poles all and returned at nite

Spent the sum of $o^{75} during the month of January

February 1872
1 Thirsday morning at Bs & went & taken Miley home & Ellen went home with her & i mailed 2 leters one to T.L. Haun and the other to E.L. Andruss & I returned here at nite & brought Rese 2 dolars worth coffe & 1&3 [illeg.] of [illeg.] cloth
    for pickels   75

2 Friday morning at Bs & bilt fence all day at the Estep place me Eli & Bud

3 Saturday morning at Bs & halled wood till noon and in the after noon me & Davy cut a beetree in the after noon

4 Sunday morning at Bs & i was sick all day i chilled on Saturday nite

5 Monday morning at Bs & i was sick all day & it is raining & Will & Serena are here

6 Tusday morning at Barrons & remained at the house all day & do N

7 Wensday morning at Bs & i washed my clothing in the forenoon & in the after noon halled hay with William & Eli skined my yearling

8 Thursday morning at Barrons & went to Mastervill & taken Ellen home & I went in the buggy & on the 7 of this month Ellen got a dress & in the evening me & Ellen got home & Davy went to Moreses for to take some corn for to take to mill & me & William went ahunting & I killed a beaf branded & marked

9 Friday morning at Bs & me & Eli & Davy went and got the beaf in the fore noon & in the after noon i finished my planter

10 Saturday morning at Bs & me & Eli planted onions till noon & in the after noon I went ahunting & killed a turkey & found a bee tree

11 Sunday morning at Bs & me & Eli & Davy went & cut a bee tree

12 Monday morning at Bs me & Eli made fence all day at the Estep Place

13 Tusday morning at Mr Bs me & Eli William halled wood till noon & in the after noon i went ahunting & killed a deer

14 Wensday morning at Mr Bs me Bud & Eli bilt fence all day

15 Thirsday morning at Bs me Bud & Eli bilt fence all day & we finished the big job

16 Friday morning at Barrons & helped in the field at the house & after noon plowed

17 Saturday morning at Barrons & went to the Estep place & raked weed and burnt them & returned to the house in the evening

18 Sunday morning at Bs & went ahunting and killed 2 turkeys & got a cow skin marked with 1 shu8t c9up 38 th2 39ta & 5-2s & 58d23 B9t 3n the left

19 monday morning at Barrons me & Williams plowed in the litte field all day

20 Tusday morning at Bs & went up the coton wood and skined a cow the rest of the day done nothing

21 Wensday morning at Bs me & William planted corn all day

22 Thirsday morning at Barrons me & William & Paw went to help survey Moreses land me & William carried the chain all day

23 Friday morning at Barrons me & William planted corn all day

24 Saturday morning at Bs me & William went to hunt for a hid & got one & returned at noon in the after noon do nothing

25 Sunday at Barrons & remained at the house all day untill noon & in the after noon me Davy & Bud went & looked for a hide & we found 2 hides & returned at dark

26 Monday at Barrons & i plowed all day at the Estep Place and in the evening I sold my hide for 19.30 to Bloomfields

27 Tusday at Barrons & plowed all day at the Estep Place

28 Wensday at Barrons me & Davy hunted cow hides all day & found 2

29 Thirsday at Barrons me Bud & Davy went & killed a beaf & got a hide the beaf was a bad beaf

Spent during the month of February the sum of $2^{00} & sold the sum of $19.30 worth of hides

March 1872
1 Friday at Barrons & remained there all day & done nothing

2 Saturday at Barrons me & William halled wood all day

3 Sunday at Barrons & helped to dig a grave & the rest of the day I stayed with Ellen

4 Monday at Barrons & remained at the house all day & done nothing

5 Tusday at Paws & went to the Estep Place & plowed all day me & Bud both

6 Wensday at Paws & went to the field & plowed all day & finished braking up my ground

7 Thirsday at Paws & went to the field and marked off my
ground 1 way & it rained nearly all day & Travis was down

8 Friday at Paws me & Bud went to Mastervill & I pade Thad
what I owed him and got 8 yards of bleached domestick
for   ~~100~~⁰⁰
for 8 yard of brown   75
for 3 yards of red calico   40
pade Thad   495
for boots

9 Saturday at Paws & in the fore noon shelled corn & in the after
noon went & marked off my ground for the plot

10 Sunday at Paws & remained at the house all day & Mr & Mrs
Moriss were there

11 Monday morning at Paws & planted corn all day for seed
corn for Mr Rese
                    for corn   50

12 Tusday at Paws and finished planting corn by noon & in the
after noon went to look for a hide & got 1 hide

13 Wensday at Paws and went to look for a hide me and Davy &
we got one & in the after noon me & Bud got 1 hide & in the
evening I received a leter from E.L. Andruss stating that Ellen
was married on February the 29

14 Thirsday at Paws & remained at the house all day and rote a
leter to E.L. Andruss ~~and to Jacob Haun~~ [scratched out] & in the
evening I received 3 dollars for hids

15 Friday at Paws & helped Bud plant untill noon and in the
afternoon plowed at the house & at nite Almeda & Mr Paterson
came

16 Saturday at Paws and went ahunting & killed a turkey before
breakfast & stayed at the house the rest of the day

17 Sunday at Paws and remained at the house all day & Paterson
& his wife started home

18 Monday at Paws and fixed to start to Waco in the evening
went as far as Thads & William & Serena went that far

19 Tusday at T Mixens & went to Waco me & Thad & bought
          for calico 10 lds & trim   1^{50}
          & for Serena 3 yds red   40
          for yellow 2 yd   25
& remained at Waco all nite

20 Wensday at Waco
          for handkercheif 2   50
& then to Thads and unloaded & then started home and got
home at nite & I received a leter from H.S. Crow dated March 2
    for stamps 10   30
    for paper   15
    for envelopes   25
    for tax   10

21 Thirsday at Paws and went to look for hides and returned at
noon & got to hides & I remained at the house the rest of the
day

22 Friday at home & remained there all day

23 Saturday at Paws and went ahunting with Davy and didnt kill
any thing and in the evening went to look for a cow and didnt
find any

24 Sunday at Paws & went to Mr Morises & then to Miss [illeg.]
and got home at nite 18d b5d 18d B366 h1d 1 f5ss

25 Monday at Paws & hawled poles untill noon & in the after
noon helped bud plant corn

26 Tueday at paws & halled wood untill noon & in the after noon
& in the after noon went shunting & seen Rese a cutting poles
this side of his track

27 Wensday at Paws & went to look for horses and went to
Masterville and got soap
          for soap   75
and Dave Mixen come and stade all nite with us

28 Thirsday at Paws & helped Bud & D Mixen make a list & in the evening rote Uncle Dick & Paw & Bill left in the buga and Dave remained with us

29 Friday at Paws & fixed the pen in the after noon & Paw & Bill returned from Powers

30 Saturday at Paws & it rained in the fore noon & in the after noon me & Bill went ahunting and marked a willd hog and Coal came to us

31 Sunday at Paws & remained at the house all day & in the evening Dave Vestel went home received 4 dolar of wood for bids Spend during the~month of March the sum $9.85 sold H9d2s 5p to th2 61st 4f 719ch to th2 17458t 4f $35.10

Aprile 1872
1 Monday at Paws & got up Biley and fixed the pen

2 Tusday at Paws & went ahunting for horses & in the morningDick broke his neck and hunted horses in the evening with Cooper & Hines and the old man left for Coals

3 Wensday at Paws & remained at the house till noon and in the after noon went ahunting & returned at nite & didnt kill any thing

4 Thirsday at Paws & remained at the house all day & Mr Cox & his wife came and stayed and it rained all day and at nite Paw came home from Powers

5 Friday at Paws & remained at the house all day & Fred Mcartney came down

6 Saturday at Paws & in the fore noon went & got up a horse & in the after noon went & got up some cows one of the H cows & fred and Bill went to Masterville & returned at nite & Travis came with them & had a spasm that nite

7 Sunday morning at Paws & remained at the house all day & Trav had to fits & in the evening Taff & his wife came down & at nite & Travis he had 2 fits

8 Monday at Paws & it rained all nite & hailed & right house blowed down & all the horses was gon from the pasture & we bilt fence all day me davy Bill & Bud boath at the house & at Estep place

9 Tusday morning at Paws & replanted my corn against noon & the rest of the boys got cut timber for the store & Rese moved in the fore noon to the White place & in the after noon I made a little gate

10 Wensday at Paws & went to look for a cow & got one of my tB cows & then went to babes & taken the clothing & the rest of the boys worked in the timber & in the after noon I worked in the timber ageting timbers for the store & Bud & Pok moved home

       for 2 drapes 10 lds in each $2^{50}

11 Thirsday at Paws & done nothing in the fore noon& in the after noon went & got the logs on the prarie & Arch Williams was here & was here all the day before

12 Friday at Paws & in the fore noon shelled corn & hoed onions & in the after noon fixed the pen

13 Saturday at home & went to clam to mill and returned at 2 ocl & the rest of the day done nothing

14 Sunday at Paws & remained at the house all day & Fred started for Waco and Trav went as far as Masterville & Bill & Serena went to Reids Bud went after Hinz and I stade at the house all day & Mr Moriss was here in the evening

15 Monday morning at home went to geting up horses & branded 5 young colts and 3 yearlings to of them had Whites brand on them & 1 had none & we got th32 thlt u18d8t b318d8d 18d w2 p5th27 38 the pasture

16 Tueday at home & gathered horses all day & branded 6 colts 1 rk & rest TH & Fred returned from Waco & Trav & Joe came with them

17 Wensday at home went to Babes in the fore noon & in the after noon plowed at the house me & Billy

       for shoes $2^{00}

18 Thirsday at Home & plowed all day at the house me & Bill & I worked Pada

19 Friday at Paws & plowed at the house all day & received a leter from home with a bill of articles & Davy started for Waco for goods i went ahunting in the morning and killed a turkey

20 Saturday at Paws & plowed all day in my corn William helped me all day & Bud went to Masterville and got the darkey & they returned at dark

21 Sunday at Paws & plowed all day & remained at the house all day & rote a leter home & the darkey road the wild yelou mar & in the evening Bud & the rest of the horse hunters returned & we branded 1 yearling 1 of the white colts

22 Monday at Paws & finished plowing my corn & in the aftere noon cut weeds & the aftere noon Wat road the sorel horse

23 Tusday at Paws & plowed all day for Bud & in the evening come by Grigs and got a cow of Paws

24 Wensday at Paws & finished plowing my corn against noon & in the aftere noon done nothing only get up the wild mair

25 Thirsday morning at Paws & shelled corn in the fore noon & in the after noon killed one of my HH yearling & it had 3 other brands on it one of them was   & on the shoulder

26 Friday morning at Paws & went to Masterville & bought
       for Bride Bits   25
       for trickery 6 yds 1^{50}
& 1 yard of camebrick & returned in the evening and [illeg.] altered a horse L.B.

27 Saturday at Paws & get up horses & altered three for LB in the fore noon & 1 for the (Sen) in the after noon

28 Sunday at Paws & remained at the house all day & Paw returned from Daan Coals where he went the day before

29 Monday at Paws & halled a load of wood in the fore noon me & wet & in the aftere noon fixed up some beagum and fixed my

log [illeg.] & Mrs Mers was there all day & William went to Masterville

30 Tueday morning at Paws & it is raining & we fixed for to start on ahunting & camped at Herels

Spent during the month of April the sum of $3.75 & Paw got to dresses that hant counted in which amounts to $250

May 1872
1 Wensday in camp at Herls & got up 4 head of horses and then drove for Patersons and there got and put in the pens & camped for the nitc & Wat road the rone that we got at Herels & Bud returned from town drunk

2 Thirsday morning at Patersons & started up the country & camped at Halcom & didnt find anything all day

3 Friday in camp at Halcoms
   for baking bread by Mrs Halcom   50
   crackers & oysters   50
at Pery & we got 4 head of horses near that place & then returned to the pen & from there to the head of the Elam & then started home in the nite

4 Saturday morning at Paws & branded 1 yearling in the HK brand & brought the sorel mar of Bud & branded her HK on the left shoulder & pade
  ten $10 for her $10^{00}
pade for sorel ~~Wat and~~ William Reid was present & remained at the house all day

5 Sunday morning at Paws & remained at the house all day & Moreses girls was here & Paw went down to the store & taken Mr Mores & Bud y4t s472 721 t 38 th2 2u2 838y

6 Monday at Paws
  for cuters   1.10
of baby Barron & then plowed all day in the field at the house & 1t 89te hld h266 w3th 15d B Reid & all the family was present

7 Tusday at Paws & plowed all day at the house & Paw returned home in the evening & Thad was with him & Mr Stone was here at nite and stade all nite

8 Wensday at Paws & plowed untill noon at the house & Thad went home in the morning & in the after noon I plowed in my corn & Judge Alton was here & stayed all nite

9 Thirsday morning at Paws & plowed in my corn & William went to help me and then helped Bud to hoe his corn

10 Friday at Paws & it is raining & in the aftere noon I plowed in my corn & Wat road the Black horse for William

11 Saturday at Paws & finished plowing my corn against noon & hoe in the after noon & Wat road Elies mar for him

12 Sunday at Paws & went to Mrs Bakers & Ellen went with me & we stade all day

13 Monday at Paws & hoed in my corn all day & at nite Peavy pened here at the pen & Wat started a horse hunting

14 Tusday at Paws & hoed in my corn all day & William went to Masterville for to get the plow sharpened

15 Wensday at Paws & hoed in my corn untill noon and finished & in the evening fixed the pig pen & Paw went to Coals to the store & returned at nite

16 Thirsday at Paws & done nothing only hoed the hedge & in the evening helped Reid work his mar & William plowed

17 Friday at Paws & went ahunting in the fore noon & cripled a turkey & a wild beef & in the aftere noon Paw went to Writs & it rained a big rain & [illeg.]

18 Saturday at Paws & help to set out Patersons plants untill noon & in the aftere noon went ahunting in the aftere noon & Davy and the chaps all went to get mulberrys & I killed a turkey & cripled and other one

19 Sunday at Paws & went to Masterville
                    for Buck shot   25
& returned at noon & fred was there & William went to Babes

20 Monday at Paws & in the fore noon got off the mare & branded a colt for Paw & in the aftere noon went ahunting and

I killed a deer & the boys came back & Trav came with them & Paw went to Coals to the store

21 Tusday at Paws & plowed all day at the in the corn me & William

22 Wensday at Paws & plowed all day in my corn & William finished the corn at the house by noon

23 Thirsday at Paws & plowed all day in my corn & Powers came here at nite with a bunch of cable & Peavy & his hands was with him

24 Friday at Paws & done nothing all day & it rained in the fore noon & John Powers started for Kansas & in the evening went ahunting & didnt kill any thing & we turned out the old mars that we had up

25 Saturday at Paws & went ahunting and didnt see any thing & at nite went to meeting

26 Sunday at Paws & went to meeting in the fore noon & the preacher came home with us Mr Cunningham Mrs Taylor Shelton & Taff & Paw braided off wild Jack for a mule & in the aftere noon we went to meeting (tuist) & they had a big time the boys allal went forward

27 Monday at Paws & started for Marlin & stopped for noon at the store at Coals & Paw went that far with me & then me & Fred went with in to mile of Marlin & ther camped

28 Tueday in camp near Marlin me & mccartney then Went into town & loaded & drove to the mill this side of the river & there camped for noon

for day book 35

& then started for the store & from there home & thad come with me & 48 61st 89t2 there was 1 b9y t372 for h5d t31e s2928& 65a all p94f2s2d

for pins 10

29 Wensday at Paws & halled a load of wood in the fore noon & Wat come home at noon & brought to mars & one colt one is said to belong to Bud & in the evening helped William to ho in the field at the house

30 Thirsday at Paws & remained at the house all day & done nothing only went ahunting in the morning & killed a deer & in the evening grained his hide he was a fine one with six points

31 Friday at Paws & in the fore noon shelled corn & in the aftere noon went to Masterville & Ellen went with me and I got some things

for boots	425
for 6 yars calico	75
for braid	10
for spool thread	10
for flanen	90
for bleached domestick	1^{00}
	35
	1^{00}

Spent during the month of May the sum of $9.90

June 1872
1 Saturday morning at Thads me & Ellen & we went home & Miley went with us we got home at noon & all the boys went to Masterville to meet the lodge & in the aftere noon I went to the field & the rest of the time done nothing & at nite I killed a wild beef marked   & branded SN

2 Sunday at Paws & remained at the house all day & the rest of them went to hear rese preach & miley was here all day

3 Monday at Paws & plowed in my corn all day & plowed the sorel mule

4 Tusday at Paws & plowed all day in my corn & Miley & her chap were here

5 Wensday at Paws & plowed all day in my corn & finished plowing my corn & miley was here & wat came from Little river

6 Thirsday at Paws & done nothing in the fore noon only killed the old bull & then killed a yearling the nite before & in the evening me & wet hoed in the corn at the house & miley went home in the fore noon William taken her home & davy huse was maried
                    HUSE

7 Friday at Paws & in the fore noon plowed the potato patch and the melon patch & fixed the milk box & in the aftere noon & the boys shelled corn for to go to mill & Travis hoed for Bud while he hunted his horse

8 Saturday at Paws & went to Elam to mill & in the after noon hoed the melon patch & sold wood my hids

for 4^{00}
& sold him paws for 5^{50}

& Wat road Travs horse & at nite he went to Moresville & it is raining at the present time & it rained all nite

9 Sunday at Paws & remained at the house all day & it misted rain nearly all day

10 Monday at Paws & went ahunting in the forenoon me & Trav & didnt kill anything but both shot at the deer down on the spring branch & at nite davy & his wife came over & stayed all nite & we set out potatoes

11 Tusday at Paws in the fore noon we went ahunting with Baby but didnt get anything & in the afternoon we done nothing & Davy went home

12 Wensday at Paws & in the forenoon went to Babes and got to cows & calfs me Travis William & Wat went aftere them & in the aftere noon we all shelled 8 bus of corn for to go to mill & davy huse wanted me to help him hoe tomorrow

13 Thirsday at Paws & me & wet helped davy huse how corn all day & trav & William went to freds to the store & they brought some boxes to go to thads

14 Friday at Paws & went ahunting in the fore noon & in the aftere noon went to look for a beef & Eli drove up one & we killed it & he taken one hind qr & William went to Masterville & returned at dark & left his horse & I got a letter from Crow & the Prcacher & to ladies came & stayed all nite & I robed a beagum in the evening

15 Saturday at Paws & went ahunting & killed a turkey & in the evening I remained at the house & the parson and his family was here & we all went to church at nite

16 Sunday at paws & went to church at Elam & there was a dispute between the preacher & thad was here & smith & I went to church at nite & Thad & Smith went home next morning

17 Monday at paws & made fence all day with Davy & wet & Parson Taylor came up to the meeting & reid professed & preacher Tompson & Jo Jackson taken super with us

18 Tusday at Paws & went to mastervill in the fore noon & bought said things

for belt for Ellen	50
for Alum	20
for Buck shot	50

& got knives & forks & cups & sosers for paw & I reseived a leter from home & they had a prar meeting here in the evening

19 Wensday at Paws & hoed potatoes in the morning & the rest of the day done nothing & at nite i went to meeting & Ellen went with me & the preachers wife was here & Jo Jacksons

20 Thirsday at paws & remained at the house all day & in the fore noon me & wat hoed corn & potatoes & they had meting here in the evening & reid & Serena stayed at the old mans

21 Friday at paws & went to mill at masterville to cons mill & returned before nite & then went to look fore a turkey & at nite Travis had to fits before dark & they went to meeting

22 Saturday at Paws & finished hawing out the corn in the fore noon & in the after noon done nothing & Travis has had 6 fits up to this time & at nite he had 2 more & me & wet went to the field to see if the hogs was geting in

23 Sunday at paws & remained at the house all day & fred & his crew was here for diner & wet went to moresville in the morning & returned at nite & the meeting brok up this evening & Parson Taylor stayed all nite

24 Monday at paws & Parson Taylor went home this morning & we done nothing all day only went to look for beef & paw whiped Serena and then made them move to reids

25 Tueday at Paws & in the fore noon went & got a little beef &

in the aftere noon we killed it & it was Paws & William came & got 1 Or of it & Wat road my fily

26 Wensday at Paws & Paw started for Waco & Wat & Bud went to freds & road the copper & I done nothing only went to Babes in the morning & in the evening cut weeds from around the fence

27 Thirsday at Paws & in the fore noon robed the bees we robed gems me & Davy & in the n Wat road Davys filet & I cut weeds & Paw was gone to Waco & Robels pened here last nite

28 Friday at Paws & finished digging the potatoes in the fore noon & the spoted houn died & Paw hant returned yet William & Gorge was here William is agoing to move to day but didnt

29 Saturday at Paws & remained at the house all day & done nothing & in the evening Paw returned from Waco & he brought some peaches with him & Travis went to the barbecue & Wat started forlitle river for to see his mother
for whiskey   50

30 Sunday at Paws & went to meeting & Taylor preached & it rained & he taken diner with us & Stevison & family & then Taylor started for home

Spent during the month of June the sum of $1^{70} and received the sum of $450

Jacksons

July 1872
1 Monday at Paws & went ahunting in the fore noon & didnt get anything onley cripled one in the afternoon done nothing & William moved to the Jacksons place to day

2 Tueday at Paws & pulled weeds in the fore noon & in the aftere noon went ahunting & killed a deer & the boys went to look for some cows of Paws & Travis went to Elam to see the doctor

3 Wensday at Paws & worked on the hack in the fore noon & in the aftere noon me & Davy went ahunting & didat see anything & Travis went to freds & got some things for William

4 Thirsday at Paws & remained at the house all day & grained a deer skin & the boys came in & they got to cows that belonged to Paw & Eli got the lisle houn (Pirg) this evening

5 Friday at Paws & went to Babes in the fore noon & in the after noon remained at the house & done nothing & Paw went to freds & back & it is raining at the present time & rained nearly all nite

6 Saturday at Paws & went ahunting in the morning me & Travis & Davy & Baby but didnt overtake us & we returned at noon & at nite Davy & Vi came over and stade all nite

7 Sunday at Paws & went to the field in the morning with Paw & Davy and returned to the house & found Shelton & his wife there & Davy and his wife stade all nite here last nite & William got 1 bushel of meal

8 Monday at Paws & me & Travis went & got a little beef of mine & returned at noon & hired Eli to cut post & then went to Morses & Baby was here when we returned & in the evening we let William get a quarter of the beef that we killed of mine

9 Tusday at Paws & went to babes & then to morses for to get him to make me a girt & Davy went to plowing & broke his plow & then went to the shop & Morses boy drove for him

10 Wensday at Paws & hoed some in the melons & Thad was here & i pade him what i owed him which was to the amount of 7 & then he went to freds Paw went to Reids & got the gruben hoe & 1 [illeg.] of ham & chains & Morses boy drove som to day & i started a leter to E.L. Andruss & at nite to preachers stade all nite Lily & Aken

11 Thirsday at Paws & went to Writs & got a yoak of cable & then me & leporde went ahunting & I killed a dear & in the evening done nothing Hix drove all day

12 Friday at Paws & plowed the potatoes in the fore noon & in the after noon done nothing & Travis came here in the evening Hix drove to day

13 Saturday at Paws & cut brush in the fore noon & in the aftere noon done nothing & davy broke his plow again & went to elam

to the shop and got it fixed & William & Serena was here to day
& he tuke his horse home & I road my filey

14 Sunday at Paws & went to Sheltons me & Ellen & we went
in the buga & davy & his wife & 0x & a boy that lives at rites

15 Monday at Paws & dressed 2 dear skins & went ahunting and
didnt kill anything & Dave Vestal was here & William taken his
hogs home & i sold Wod Broomfield to hids
     for 2^{25}
& the boy comenced to drive to day

16 Tusday at Paws & went to the field in the morning & in the
evening i dressed a dear skin & taken the clothes to Babes & the
boy is driving to day & Bud & William went to hunt for cows on
Pan Creek & they returned & got none & William got a can of
soap this evening & the boy is driving all day

17 Wensday at Paws & went to the field in the morning &
William cut brush all day & Mr Crutch field was here & Paw
started for Wacoithis evening & the boy is driving all day

18 Thirsday at Paws & went to Babes and then went ahunting &
didnt see any thing & William & Serena is here & he [illeg.] the
plow & the boy drove & Cooper & his hands was here

19 Friday at Paws & went ahunting in the fore noon & Bud killed
a deer & the boy drove all day

20 Saturday at Paws & went to Babes & got the clothes &
William got a ~ bushel of meal & I went & got the mashene in
the evening but I didnt get it i left it this side of maxes branded
5 yong colts & to counter Br of T39 & 1 yearling

21 Sunday at Paws & remained at the house & me & Davy went
and got some melons

22 Monday at Paws & started for Marlin & got as far as the store
& then turned back Fred had got a wagon & then i returned
home & the boy drove all day
     for pants 2^{25}

23 Tusday at Paws & went to the field & there found the cattle

in & returned & in the aftere noon bought of Bud his intrast in the sorel for $10.00 & Wat & William Reid was present at that time I went & got the mashine & Bud went to Outing poles & Paw went to Bets on Elam & returned at noon & the boy drove all day

Ellen   E   Lord

My   My   My Dear

savoy

J.H Taliues
Eagle Springs
  Coriel Co

A R all was 4/5 are all under 4 years 250

salt 1 barel
flour
meat
calico 4 Ids
shugar

On opposite page: *A page from J. L. Courtney's diary shows the code he often used. On the page he inadvertently signed his name, "J. James."*

Below: *Enlargement of signature from that page.*

W.M. Roberts

John Hitson & Bill Palapinto
Stephenvill texas

William Gordang
lives on the Colorado R.
one stack from Stephenvill
to Colorado R.

W.L. Painter lives in Stephenvill

Le Varnan lives in Stephenvill

G.L. Robinson h5fflke9j
c629k 5 8te8 H97ts

Gorge Shillmind

Beada lives 1 milesouth of Decator

W.S. Wallace
lives 2 miles north of Decator

J.H. Practor lives 1 mile north of
Decator

William Parsion lives 2 mile south of
Decator

James Harding lives in Decatur

Cournal Pickit
lives 4 miles north east
of Decatur

Pam Wagner lives in Decatur

McConell lives in Balius

Newman & Co lives near Fort Worth

B.F. Phelps
Blanco Co. Blanco town
10 miles North East

Jack Matheth lives on Mustang Cr

B.M.L. Davis
New Albany Kansas

W. Obryan
Anerson PO
Grimes Co Texas

Edward Sunderland
Delavan Tazewll Co.
Ill

John Geeley
Mustang Creek
Gildeon

Chatman an Gilamore
William
Watson lives on
Mustang Cr

Cage lives in
Stephenvill

Clehan County seat
Jackson County

J. Walker
Clifton Bosque Co.

Henry Crawfield
lives on South
Bosque

Ross lives on Leon

J. Odel lives on Ha
Buck

G. Millmind

Robert Cates at
Decatur TX
Albert Crosgrove
Wisconsin

Thomas Barron lives
in Deer Creek

H.H. Andruss
Bryan City Texas

Edward Pawson
Delaware Tazewell Co
Illinois

[24, 25, 26, 27, 28, 29 missing]

30 Tusday in camp on the head of deer creek acuting hay for Eliet & cut hay all day & Eliet halled one load & raked about half [illeg.] & I camped in the prarie by myself & I cut about 6 acars to day

31 Wensday in camp [illeg.] acuting hay for Eliet & cut 4 acers and a ½ & camped in the [illeg.] & [illeg.] hailing hay

Spent during the month of July the sum of $2^{35}
I received the sum of $225 from Wad for hides I sod him

August 1872
1 Thirsday morning in camp in the prarie acuting hay for Eliet & finished cutting by ten oclock & then went to cut hay for Persell & cut 3 acres for him & then went to cut hay for [illeg.] & returned to my old camp & to felows camped with me

2 Friday in camp in the [illeg.] & cut hay for Brewer cut him 1 acre and 3 [illeg.] & then moved 1½ mile up the creek & cut him three acers & ¼ & they all settled with me Persell pade me four & ¼ dolars Eliet pace me seven dolars & ½ and then I loaded & started for home & got home at nite & Paw give me sixteen dolars for what I done for [illeg.]
      from Paw received $16^{00}

3 Saturday at Paws & went ahunting & didnt see anything & Paw went to freds & got me a net
      for net
      for (ribets)   50
& he returned at nite & Jo Mores was here & got a sack of peaches Wat went off to Masterville

4 Sunday at Paws & went to meting to hear Parson Taylor & he taken diner with us & Stevison & William & Serena is here she is agoing to stay here awhile & Poca is sick & rese was here to day wet hant returned yet

5 Monday at Paws & went to cutting hay & Shelton Axed & William all was here they didn't do anything only shelton made a rake in the evening

6 Tusday at Paws & cut grass untill noon & in the aftere noon killed a beef & the boys halled all day Shelton maxey Wat & William

7 Wensday at Paws & cleaned out the spring in the fore noon & in the aftere noon I cut hay & went & got Mrs Baker & the boys halled hay all day Shelton Willy maxey & Wat & Davy & the boy has plowed all this week

8 Thirsday at Paws & halled hay untill noon & in the aftere noon I cut hay & cuningham halled 25 acers of grass & rese halled 2 acers & mores halled 1 load to day & the boy drove to day & Mrs Baker is here to day & nite & wet started for Belton this morning before day & William helped to day & Bud to

9 Friday at Paws & cut hay all day & mores halled hay all day & William & Bud halled hay & Shelton raked hay all day davy & the boys plowed all day & quit plowing for the present & Paw pade John 5 dolars & still oes him 3 dolars and Johns time is up for the present

10 Saturday at Paws & stacked hay & mores & William & Bud is hailing hay & Shelton is raking & Shelton finished raking by noon & Mrs Baker went home this morning and Paw went with her & in the evening I went & got the meal & Mrs Baker

11 Sunday at Paws & wet came in & his wife is at Babes & mrs Baker is here & Serena & William is here & thcy have been here every since last Sunday & wet Brought his wife over to day & he moved in the house with bud & there was a crowd here for diner (Jo) Adams had his things brought up to day from Mrs Gallaway

12 Monday at Paws & in the forenoon went & cut 2 acers of grass for Rese & in the evening helped to server out mine & Buds land we serveyed the prarie part of the land & the timber is to server yet McGey serveyed the land for us & Paw went to Mastersville in the fore noon

13 Tusday at Paws & went & cut Williams hay & then went to cutting for Baby & at noon I went to moreses & got my diner & ground the sicle & William raked his hay to day & Mrs Baker went home this morning she was here just a weake

14 Wensday at Paws & went to cutting hay for Boby & cut him 3 acers & then cut 2 acers for Bud Galaway & then taken the mashene down to Mrs Bakers & it rained & I had to come home & it is raining know & William and Shelton halled hay while it rained

15 Thirsday at Paws & went ahunting in the fore noon with Thad William & Bud & in the aftere noon went & cut hay for cuning-ham & in the fore noon I loaned Paw five dolars for to get a sack of salt

16 Friday at Paws & went to get Mrs Baker & I remained at the house all day & davy went & cut hay & Paw went to the store down to freds & I mended my boots & Ellens shuse & at nite the first girl was borned & ant saryann was here

17 Saturday at Paws & went & taken mrs Baker home & I pade her for her service
        for midwife per   5.00
& then went home & went & killed a beef & it was branded 30 & a read brand 7u & Wat helped me & davy cut Sheltons hay & finished by noon & in the evening I received a leter from home & the quilt patern & Wad sent & got the hide by Davy & [illeg.] got a quarter of beef

18 Sunday at Paws & Thad & Smith & there family & stade all day & malisa was here to & I rote a leter home & sent it to office by Thad

19 Monday at Paws & went to moreses & ground to sicles & then returned home & in the morning I pade Serena for her work
        for Serenas work   250
& Bud Wat & John went to gathering corn in the little field at the house & davy went to cut hay for mores

20 Tusday at Paws & we gathered corn all day in the field at the house Bud Wat & John helped to gether the corn & we gathered four loads of corn & at nite davy & Vi was here & galaway came here & got a steer & Harriet washed all day

21 Wensday at Paws & Vi Huse is here & stayed all day & to mrs galaways and to Mrs Bakers was here to & davy cut hay for mores & me & Bud & wet finished gathering corn here [illeg.] noon & at nite turned the hogs in the field & davy has been here every nite since he has been cutting hay & I tied mrs Baker a [illeg.] & Johnny started to pick coten

22 Thirsday at Paws & halled corn from [illeg.] [illeg.] all day me & wet & davy cut hay for mores & [illeg.] is here we halled to loads before noon & to in the evening & Bud worked at his

crib & davy finished by noon for mores & he has worked with the (illeg.) 4 days 1 day for cuningham & Shelton & 3 days for mores & brought mashene home at noon

23 Friday at Paws & Paw went down to the store & me & davy halled poles to make a shed in the fore noon and in the aftere noon we mooved a crib from Bill Rites & Bud went to mill & Vi is here & Paw returned from the store in the evening & davy & Vi is here & stade all nite & Bud returned from mill at dark

[24 , 25, 26, 27 missing]

28 Wensday at Paws & halled corn for Bud till noon & I worked his mair we halled to loads in the fore noon & in the aftere noon we worked (illef.) & coperhead & we halled one load for Bud & Wat helped all day & in the evening we halled one load from Elis

29 Thirsday at Paws & Paw started for Waco & me & Bud & wet gathered corn untill noon & in the aftere noon we halled corn & we halled one load from Elis & we finished felling Buds corn in the evening & fealled 8 rows [illeg.] & davy huse killed his steer & let me kep 1 for qr for the one he got of me

30 Friday at Paws & halled to loads of corn in the fore noon for Bud & one in the aftere noon & finished [illeg.] corn for Bud & [illeg.] from Hariet

31 Saturday at Paws & gathered in my corn & we gathered 3 loads & Bud & Wat helped me all day & has been gone to Waco three days to day & some time during the month between the 15 & twenty fifth I let davy have one dolar for to get some tobaco & Johnny came here this evening

    Huse $1^{00}

Spent during the month of August the sum of $8^{00}
& Reseived the sum of $20

September 1872
1 Sunday at Paws & went to meeting to heare Parson Taylor & Davy pade me what he owed me which was

    res $1.00
& I got a book from Taylor
    for book   25

& Jo Adams came up here this morning & Wat went to masterville & Johnny is here & Paw came home at noon from Waco &
Parson Allen & Jones was here at nite

2 Monday at Paws & went to gather my corn & gathered 1 load
in the forenoon & Paw went down to the store & Bud & wet
helped to gather corn & we gathered to loads & finished my corn
I had nine loads of corn & 16 bushel to the load & Paw came
back from the store & brought Buton with him

3 Tusday at Paws & went & got the rest of the rent from Eli
which was 40 bushel & mores is hailing his rent he has halled 2
loads which makes 54 bushel & davy got the horses this morning to go to gathering his corn & in the aftere noon me & Paw
& Wat went to rites & got some logs & then fixed the spring &
cleaned it out

4 Wensday at Paws & Paw pade me the five dolars that he got to
get the salt with & he started for Waco this morning & I fixed
my [illeg.] & last nite I (code)
                    for money owed   5.00
& pade this morning & (code) in the evening I killed a beef
branded L3 & marked [illeg.] & reses went to getting corn &
bud helped him & mores finished hailing his rent to day only
three bushel

5 Thirsday at Paws & stayed at the house all day & barbecued
the meat & davy halled eleven bushel of his rent corn this morning the corn from Elis & Paw is gone to Waco & Wat done nothing all day only helped me to cut up the meat & at nite Paw came
home from Waco & he brought Jo Adams & Serena a dress a
Pease & some apels & Hariet washed to day

6 Friday at Paws & we gathered Reses corn which was 3-loads
which made 48 bushel & Paw went down to the store & he got
Jeckens & Coals coten & he returned at nite & William was here
to day & he got check wat helped all day
    for soap for to wash baby shaving soap   25

7 Saturday at Paws & we drove all the cattle up to the field to
water & we watered the cows & a darky came to see wat from
Little rivers & wat went to moreses & got to bushel of meal & at
nite Jonney came

8 Sunday at Paws & I went over to the north west corner of my
land & put a rock up there marked [illeg.] & Johnny is here &
wet went to masterville & I sold wet my hide

for sold 2^{75}

& Johney went back to pick coten & William & Serena & davy
got his rooster & Thad was here and stayed all day

9 Monday at Paws & fixed the wagon for to go to halling coten
& bud (code) & Paw went to maxes & to moreses & in the
evening I killed to turkeys & at nite thad came down

fore a dress dolar and 1^{25}

for Winslow soothing soap   35

10 Tusday at Paws & me & Thad went down to coals & got to
loads of cotton & taken it [illeg.] Reses & there left it on the far
bank of the (Ha Lior) & then we came home & stayed there &
Bud started for Waco this morning & he went there for the purpose of getting some land in the sedor Brake

11 Wensday at Paws & me & Thad went to hour wagons down
by Reses & then to coxes and unloaded and then back home &
then down to the coton pile & I pad thad for to dolar [illeg.]
dress & the winslows soap

12 Thirsday at Coals & me & Thad went from the coton pile to
the Jin & unloaded & then back to Thads & stayed all nite

13 Friday at Thads & then came home & Thad went aftere a
load of coten & there was a man here last nite & he had a dead
sined & Ellen witnessed the dead & Wat & davy went to little
Elam to mill & then returned at nite & Bud returned from Waco
this evening & he said that he cut a set of [illeg.] while he was
there & they boried woods wagon for to go to mill in

14 Saturday at Paws & remained at the house all day & wet went
& taken the wagon home & he pace mores to bushel of meal that
we had got of him & William & Johnny is here & William got 1½
bushel of meal & he started back to the camp & Johney stade
here & in the evening Paw went to moreses & Bud went to braid
for a yoak of steers & Paw let him have the big wagon for one
hundred bushel of corn & Paw settled with wet this morning &
gave him & order for goods to masterville to the amount of
12.00 which is all that he oes him & wife & wet went in the
evening & returned at nite Johney is here to nite

15 Sunday at Paws & remained at the house all dayl& Bud counter branded the dun mar & in the evening he started for Waco & Wat went to moreses & got the pitch forks & there was a swarm of bees come here to day

16 Monday at Paws & Paw started for Waco & me & wet fixed the hay stack in the fore noon & in the aftere noon Wat went to Moresville & I went over on the halios & killed to coons & Wat road the mare & Ellen & Jo went to griges in the buga & in the evening the horses got away my mar & coperhead

17 Tusday at Paws & went to look for the horses in the fore noon & didat find them & I killed to more coons & at nite wet came home & Paw is goan to Waco & the thing is here to nite

18 Wensday at Paws & halled corn all day from Buds crib we halled four loads me & Wat & Paw is still at Waco yet & Shelton & family is here to nite & Hariet washed to day & the thing is here & has been all day & there is a heard of cattle pened here to nite & I sold Persell some corn to the amount of
    sold corn   75

19 Thirsday at Paws & Paw is still at Waco & me & Wat finished halling the corn to day & three loads of poals against noon & in the after noon we put up the hay pens & Shelton & family is here & have been here all day & Hariet washed for them & Shelton & family went home this evening

20 Friday at Paws & he is still at Waco & in the morning I went ahunting & didut kill anything & wet went off this morning & road the mare without any leaf & he returned at nite & Brought a [illeg.] fore to take his wife off on & in the evening Ellen Jo & Poke went down to Reses & they got some (cushon)

21 Saturday at Paws & Paw is still at Waco & I halled a load of wood in the morning & then I went to Masterville
    for Bleached domestick four yards   50
& i met Paw this side of Masterville & Brought of (Biliford)
        to & ½ yards of shamey for   60
and then got a box of pills
        for mary for pills   25
        for Balmeral shirt   1^{50}
& in the aftere noon Paw came home from Waco & Dan coal &

Dave mixon got home some to or three days ago from Kansas & Johnney is here to nite & the nigers moved to day & Mrs Thread Gill died last nite

22 Sunday at Paws & Paw is gone down to Coals & Wat was here this morning & Johnny is here Wat went back to moresville & Johney stayed here all nite & Paw came home at nite & he got a draft of five hundred dolars of Dan Coal & Shelton & family camped at the spring to nite

23 Monday at Paws & fixed the fence this morning & Shelton & family is camped at the spring & Johney went back to the coten patch & Paw went to moreses & (m) & came home with paw & in the evening I went Ahunting a turkey at dark Thad came down & he brought me a letter from E.L. Andruss & I worked on the hack to day part of the day & Thad came here at dark & stayed all nite

24 Tusday at Paws & Paw went down to the store & Thad went with him & me & mores striped the hack wheels & to of the wagon wheels against noon & in the evening I put the cover on the hack & put it on ready for raining & Snotgrass is here to nite & Paw & Thad came from the store

25 Wensday at Paws & snotgrass got the wagon this morning & I went to look for a beef & I killed a turkey & then got & ARO beef & killed it & Shelton helped me & in the evening Paw went down to mrs Galaways & Thad went home this morning 26 Thirsday at Paws & Paw went to Masterville & returned at nite & in the morning I sold galaway the ARO hide for Paw & Shelton got his horses to day & I fixed the cow Pen & Johney come home to day & William moved up to the old mans from the coten patch

27 Friday at Paws & me & Johney went ahunting & I killed a coon & William & Serena was here to day & davy came & got some plank for to fix his house & Shelton & family is here yet & Serena got her broom & Bud is still at Waco aworking on his house & at nite he returned from Waco

28 Saturday at Paws & Paw went down to the store & returned at noon & Wat was here to day & I worked on the fence at the stable & Bud went to Reses to get him to moove him & I loned

William my sadle & Eli was here Shelton & [illeg.] is here yet & Eli killed one of the ARO beefs & Johney brought to mule & my saddle home in the evening & Bud bough) some wagon [illeg.] of gipson

29 Sunday at Paws & we are afixing to start for Waco & we went as far as Thads & there we stayed all nite

30 Monday at Thads me & Maw & Ellen & we stayed all day

for garters   15

for [illeg.] & stamps   5

& I pade 65 cts for a dress for Jo out of maws money & we remained at Thads all day & nite & Thad went & got his wagon for to go aftere a load of coten to [illeg.] [illeg.] & to go to the lower store to get a lot of millinery

Spent during the month of September the sum of $4.65 & Reseived the sum of $ 4.50

October 1872

1 Tueday at Thads me & Ellen & Maw & Curg & Lue & we went from there to Patersons & there stayed all nite & I bought of Thad a shall

for a [illeg.] shall   450

& Thad started after a load of coten down to Stevensons & when we got to Patersons he was gone to Coriel County

2 Wensday at Patersons & me & Ellen & Lue & [illeg.] went into town & I got

for pictures for   50

and I got some apels

for   35

& we went to obrien for diner & in the aftere noon we went down to the galery & we had 4 pictures for the baby & 4 for Ellen & 4 more for me and they all came to

amt 1^{25}

& at nite we returned to Patersons & there stayed all nite & those pictures that we had taken was taken by Mr Bolton & I Bought

to yards of calico for   25

3 Thirsday at Patersons & we all went into town to Obrians & stayed there for diner & then we went down to galery & I [illeg.] of Ellens pictures taken

for pictures   50

for cake   15

& then we went to Mr Stons & there stayed all nite

4 Friday at Mr Stones & me & curg-went down in town & he had his

for curgs picture	50
and I got some calico & Butens	50
for apels for curg	10

& we remained at Stons untill noon & in the aftere noon we went to Obrians & there stayed all nite & Obrian wasant at home he left home to day & no one knows where he went

5 Saturday at Obrians

for painkillers	25
for flour	25

& I pade 1^{25} of maws money for nails for Thad   50

for mackerel for Miley   75

cents worth & then we hitched up & started for home & went out as far as Patersons and stayed there untill aftere noon & then we hitched up & went to Thads & there stayed all nite & I pace Thad what I owed him

for shall $450

6 Sunday at Thads & I got maw a Balmoral & a botle of medicine & then we started for home & we got home at noon & Shelton & Bud killed a beef one of the ARO yearling & at nite Reses wagon came to moove Bud

7 Monday at Paws & Bud started to moove to Waco this morning & I went ahunting & didn't kill anything & davey went to the store aftere the wagon but didnt get anything & returned at nite & Paw sold galaway his hid for $1.40 & Shelton helped Bud to moove & in the evening I fixed the doors I sawed off of the midle dors of the smoke house

8 Tuaday at Paws & fixed the fence at the yard & then went ahunting and killed to coons & in the fore noon I killed a wild guss

9 Wensday at Paws & cut 3 acers of grass for davy Huse & Paw went down to the store & Johney raked hay for davy & davy worked the oxens & Paw returned from the store at nite & Robeles pened some cattle here & I sold them one bushel of corn for 50 c & Johney started for the coten patch this evening

10 Thirsday at Paws & I went ahunting & killed to turkeys &

Shelton returned from Waco from moving Bud & the to maxes was here this evening

11 Friday at Paws & I went and got the wagon & Brought a load of corn back with me I went down to the widow lees & got a load of corn and I eat diner with gorge Austin & the rest of the coten pickers & I got home at nite & Shelton helped me unload the corn & Shelton traided wagons with galaway, John

12 Saturday at Paws & me & Davy & William killed a cow [code] & William got Buster to take his home & davy got the wagon & Shelton went aftere a load of rock up on Deer Creek & in the evening Paw went up to Reids

13 Sunday at Paws & cut up the beef & put it out to cook & Thad came down & William Brought Old Buster home & Bud galaway was here & Old man Reid & I remained at the house all day & tended to my beef & Jo went to mrs galaways to day

14 Monday at Paws & went to cut hay for Maxey & I cut five acers for him & returned at dark
15 Tusday at Paws & Paw & Shelton went down to the store & I sold Wood a hide
        for sold $400
and I pade davy for breaking the mar I pace him
        pade Huse $1^{00}
& then I went & halled a load of wood & Ellen & Jo went to see Serena & returned at nite & Paw returned at nite & I traided one of my pistols to Wood for his rifle

16 Wensday at Paws & halled 2 loads of wood in the fore noon & in the aftere noon I hung the crib [illeg.] & cripled a wild goose & Shelton mooved home to day he got abarel here & Serena & William is here to nite & there was some Pelters here to this evening

17 Thirsday at Paws & went Ahunting & didnt see anything & William taken his hogs home this morning in the wagon & I smoked my deer skin & at nite I sold calwell 3 bushel of corn
        sold   1^{50}
and he camped at the spring & davys plowing he (P) to day

18 Friday at Paws & Paw went to Masterville & returned at nite
& he got 4 yards of flanen for the baby
            which cost   30 cts
per yard & he didnt charge me anything for it & Johney came up
& stade all nite & in the evening I killed a deer & Johney was
with me & davy plowed all day & in the fore noon I worked at
my buck skins

19 Saturday at Paws & Paw went down to the store & returned
at nite & I finished dressing 2 of my buck skins & Johney started for the coten patch this morning & davy didnt plow to day he
went to the blacksmith shop & I grained to Buck skins one that
I killed last fall & the one that I killed a friday nite

20 Sunday at Paws & Wood came & got his hide this morning
& I cant by him for some Buck shot & then me maw curk &
Ellen went down to davy & came back by noon & davy& vi came
home with us & they went home at nite & Taff was here in the
evening & snotgrass came and got the wagon in the evening &
Jo went home with Taff for to stay to or three weeks

21 Monday at Paws & me & Paw went & got some timber for to
make ax hoes & I killed to turkeys & in the evening we made 4
hoes & at nite Wood came by & got the pistol that I traided to
him for his rifle & I smoked to deer skins this evening & davy
went to the blacksmith shop & he taken the ARO brand for Paw
& Ellen loned old mrs write her saddle & in the evening wood
returned from marlin & brought me some shot
            for buckshot   50

22 Tusday at Paws & I went Ahunting & killed a deer & given
half of it to Will Baron & then I came home & staked off the
ground for davy to plow & William was here in the evening &
got a mess of venesen

23 Wensday at Paws & went to babes & then went to moreses &
got my gun that I got of Wood & then back to Babes & got diner
& then home & grained a deer skin & I lost my picket roap to
day Rite Brought Ellens sadle home & taken my rifle to [illeg.]
& broke the old tube off Sal had a gal

24 Thirsday at Paws & went ahunting & didnt kill anything but
I found my picket roap & Paw went down to Maxes in the
evening & Ellen got scared & went to hunt for me but I beat her
home

25 Friday at Paws & washed to of my deer hids & Maxey got the oxens & moreses got some salt 13 pound & Serena was here Ellen washed

26 Saturday at Paws & Paw went down to the store & me & Jim Maxey cleaned out the well in the fore noon & in the aftere noon I went up to Reids & got some grapes &timber to make some ax handles & to look for my houn but didant find he left last Monday Johney came up this evening

27 Sunday at Paws & remained at the house all day William & Serena was here to day & Thad was here & I received a leter from Home & I answered it today & Ellen wrote a leter to Mary Jane to day & we sent them to the office by Thad & Will Baron pade me
Pade to Paw   3⁵⁰

28 Monday at Paws & Paw went down & bought Maxes coten & Maxey came home with him & davy went to get the big wagon & in the evening I went to look for a cow & got wet & snot-grasses came & brought a sack of flour

29 Tusday at Paws & Paw went down to the store & back at nite & I went to help snotgrass get up some horses they got to fidls & chuck & in the afternoon went ahunting Eliets was here to go ahunting (William) went with me & William pade us ½ bushel of meal that he owed

30 Wensday at Paws & Paw went down to Mrs Galaways & I fixed the chimney hole at the kitchen & davy is plowing part of to day moreses & Maxey was here

31 Thirsday at Paws & Paw went to Masterville & he brought me a check of 50 dolars from home & I remained at the house & didnt do anything only patch the brush fence davy is plowing maw finished my buckskin pants today Willey Baron pade 1.00 dollar which was all he owed me for cutting hay & I give all the money that he has pade me to Paw which was $4⁵⁰

Spent during the month of October the sum of $11¹⁰
& received the sum of $3.00

November 1872

1 Friday at Paws & Paw went down to the store & Maxey came & got some bords he got 6 hundard & I give him eight dolors of Paws money & that was all he owed him for his coten & I went ahunting & William came to me & I didnt kill anything William & Serena is here & [illeg.] Huse & davy is plowing

2 Saturday at Paws & me & William went to mrs nolens aftere some cows & we stayed there all nite

3 Sunday at mrs nolens & we got to cows & started for home we got to darkys to help us drive cattle we got home about to oclock Old Reid was here & Paw went to Moreses & Aunt Sary Ann lost her child day before yesterday Jo came back

4 Monday at Paws & I killed a shoat the use to belong to Bud & In the evening Ellen went down to see Aunt Saryann & I ground the sosage & salted the meet & Robert Moar was here in the fore noon

5 Tusday at Paws & I went to the timber & cut some logs for to build a stable & Ellen went down to Shelton & Mrs Maxey went with her & at nite to of the snotgrasses came here & stayed all nite

6 Wensday at Paws & I went ahunting with to of Babes boys Jim (p) and William & we didant kill anything & Snotgrass went home this morning & quit hunting horses

7 Thirsday at Paws & cut brush all day & davy plowed & snotgrass bought fidles home & chuck came home last nite & William taken his cow & calfs home to day & we branded them & I branded the one that Paw give me

8 Friday at Paws & went ahunting with Eliet & didnt kill any thing & went & boried Reids brand ax & Johney came home to day & Jo moved to Taffs & Eli was here in the evening & I sold Wood the hide that I taken off of the yerlin in the spring branch

9 Saturday at Paws & in the fore noon I went up to the Bill rites place & got some rock for to fix the chimney & in the aftere noon I fixed the fire place & old man snotgrass was here & Johney went up to [illeg.] Rites

10 Sunday at Paws & stayed at the house untill noon & William & Serena came & Shelton was up & in the evening Johney came back from [illeg.]

11 Monday at Paws & Me & Johney halled logs for to build a stable in the fore noon & in the aftere noon we put it up & Paw went & traided sows with old man Reid & davy plowed all day Maxey

12 Tusday at Paws & I cut brush untill & Maxey came & he helped me cut the brush & Dan Coal was here & in the evening me Dan & Jim Maxey all went ahunting & Dan killed a wild cat & Jim shot at a deer & davy plowed all day & Johney went to Masterville

13 Wensday at Paws & me & Jim cut post all day & we halled to loads of wood one at noon & the other at nite

14 Thirsday at Paws & me & Jim split post all day & we halled to loads of wood we split 250 post

15 Friday at Paws & we killed a hog & then went & taken the old sow to Reids & got the one that he let us have for his old one

16 Saturday at Paws & me & Jim went & got some logs for to fix the kitchen against noon & in the aftere noon I reached the mule & Jim went home

17 Sunday at Paws & remained at the house all day & Johney is sick & Ellen (on a pout) & at nite Jim came back for to work & I sold Wood a hid for
$$\text{sold} \qquad 1^{50}$$

18 Monday at Paws & me & Jim killed to hogs & Paw sold Jim the mule for 75 dolars & Bill taken him home this evening

19 Tusday at Paws & me & Jim fixed the kitchen & sawed out the core of my stable & William & Serena was here & I killed a deer this morning & give Grigs 1 qr for to drag it to the house for me & at nite Jim went down home & he road Old John & my saddle & returned in the nite awhile

20 Wensday at Paws & I halled post all day I halled to loads &

halled 240 post & Jim cut post all day Johney he chilled to day & he has had to chills before this one today & Shelton went to Masterville & back to day

21 Thirsday at Paws & I halled post all day & Jim made post all day & in the morning Wood brought Paw a sack of salt & a post auger & he brought me some wool

    for wool 1^{00}

& the Bakers outfit mooved out today

22 Friday at Paws & me & Jim halled the Reid pen to fix the field & John went down to the store & Thad came back with him & Paw went over to Bakers & I loned Wood

    loaned Wood 5^{00}

dolars & Malica had a baby & at nite Mr Baker came

23 Saturday at Paws & me & Jim halled three rails from Griges & then halled the floor out of the Reid house

24 Sunday at Paws & I went over to moreses & got the wool the wool brought me from Marlin & then I came back by Babes & Baby give me his [illeg.] & in the evening William & Serena came here & stayed all nite & to men from Waco ahunting horses & at nite Jim came back

25 Monday at Paws & I halled rails & Posts all day & some one set the prarie afire up at the uper field & jim cut post all day

26 Tusday at Paws & cut and split post all day me &Jim & Davy plowed & John drove for him

27 Wensday at Paws & we killed to hogs & davy quit plowing in the fore noon he broke the plow & there was some horses pened here the OD stock [illeg.] was gathering them & I sold him a bushel of corn

    for 1 bushel of corn   75

28 Thirsday at Paws & halled a load of wood in the fore noon & at noon I mashed my fingers & in the evening I halled a load of wood &'at nite Miss galaway & frank came here & stayed all nite & Jim split post all day & John went & taken the cloth to Miss [illeg.] this morning

29 Friday at Paws & I went to moreses to get my boots that Wood got for me

for Boots 4^{75}

& he pade me 25 cts that was all that he owed me of the five dolars that he borowed of me & then I went ahunting all day with jim Parker & Bill Barron & [illeg.] & maxey shelled corn all day

30 Saturday at Paws & I went to mill to Huses mill & Jim cut post all day & I got back at dark

Spent during the month of November the sum of $5.75 I received the sum of $2.25

December 1872
1 Sunday at Paws & in the evening Ellen went down to Griges & Lue & Vi went with her & at nite Jim came back & John went down to cows & back in the evening

2 Monday at Paws & I halled post all day & Jim made post all day & Bill Barron & Jim Parker went to work amaking rails & Baby & Tim was here & ground there axes & left the houn for me

3 tusday at Paws & I halled Post untill noon & in the aftere noon me & John went to look for some bees & Paterson came down at nite and jim cut post all day & Bill & Jim Parker cut untill noon & then quit

4 Wensday at Paws & we marked & Branded the cows & Paterson started for home & Jim went to spitting post & I went to bum around the field & John went to Masterville & back & he brought Ellen a leter from Mary Jane & the Maxey girls was up to see us

5 Thirsday at Paws & I halled post untill noon & in the after noon fixed the fence at the house & tryed to boor post holes & couldnt & Jim finished making the post today

6 Friday at Paws & me Jim & John fixed the fence at the Estep place & I killed a turkey & Mrs Baker & Dave was here all day

7 Saturday at Paws & I went & fixed fence at the rite field untill noon & then went ahunting with Eliet & I killed a deer & they killed a wolf & Jim worked all day at the fence 8 Sunday at Paws

& me & Ellen & Serena went up to mr taffs & at nite lue Hater
& family came down & Jim came back this evening & Bill rent-
ed some of the sod land

9 Monday at Paws & me & Hater hunted all day and didnt see
anything & Jim & John halled wood all day & Haters family
remained at the house all day

10 Tuesday at Paws & Hater & family is here & it is raining &
rained last nite & in the evening Hater killed deer

11 Wensday at Paws & me & Hater went ahunting & hater
cripled a deer & I killed watch & we returned at dark
12 Thirsday at Paws & we killed hogs & in the aftere noon me
& Hater went ahunting & didant see anything & John & Jim
made fence & John hired to go over the river for Bill Rite

13 Friday at Paws & me & Jim built fence all day at the rite field
& lue Hater started for home this morning & Hater let me have
his dog & [illeg.] to [illeg.]

14 Saturday at Paws & remained at the house all day & it rained
all day & at nite Dan K rite pened some horses here

15 Sunday at Paws & remained at the house all day & Rite and
his hands stayed here all day & nite
                    Grigs

16 Monday at Paws & we halled wood all day & rite started for
home & i shot at a deer a big buck & grigs he skined the bull

17 Tusday at Paws & we halled a load of wood & then it rained
all day & we remained at the house all day & Wood & Jo went
to Parson Taylors for to get married

                    Wood Broomfield

18 Wensday at Paws & we resalted the meat & then went to set-
ting post but couldnt set them & then we went & staked fence at
the rite place & we skined a cow & Jim went home at nite &
Wood & Jo was married at Taylors

19 Thirsday at Paws & went & skined a cow and Jim returned at
2 act in the evening & Paw said

        Trav got of [illeg.] $30
&
of stone & never accounted to him for it $20

20 Friday at Paws & we killed to hogs & Wood came & got the
plank to go in the floor & he mooved in the evening & Baby was
here in the evening & Bill Maxey & a boy & I sold wood to hides
for 6 dolars & Jim is to have 1^{50} of the money

21 Saturday at Paws & me & Jim cut stakes all day & William &
Serena was here all day

22 Sunday at Paws & me & Paw started for Waco & went to
Thads & got diner & then to Patersons

        for a hat of Thad 1^{75}
& stayed all nite at Patersons & we taken a horse to Waco for Dr
[illeg.]

23 Monday at Patersons & then me & Paw went into Waco &
Paterson went with us

for book day	50
for sack of shot	3.50
for tubs to	50
for hickry 10 yds	2.00
for dress 10 yds	1.25
for shews to par	

& then i got the money and my draft & got 44^{25}

        received 44^{25}
& then we came back to Pattersons and stayed all nite

        for to par of iron   1.75

24 Tusday at Pattersons & had to stay there all day for it was so
cold that we could not travel & we stayed there all day & it was
very cold all day

25 Wensday at Pattersons & we started for home & Mr Phelps
started also at the same time we did & we went to Thads for
diner & I bought some things

        for flaners for sack 1^{10}
        for linen   30
        for candy 1 P of Thad   40
& I got some paper & some spice for Maw & in the after noon
we went on home & Bud & Poca came down

26 Thirsday at Paws & went ahunting with Bud & Johney & in the evening I went over on the Indian grave branch & skined a cow & Jim wt home & I let Serena have
        for shews for   200

27 Friday at Paws & halled to loads of wood & then skined to cows & then pened to cows for to mark & Jim hant come back yet & Bud & Poca is here to nite

28 Saturday at Paws & skined a calf & then went over to [illeg.] & killed a coon & skined one of my cows & in the evening I skined a big beef & Rese & family is here

29 Sunday at Paws & remained at the house all day & Bud & Poca is here yet & Bud went down to Reses & stayed all day & at nite he returned & Jim has bin gone for four days up to this time out of his time

30 Monday at Paws & started aftere a load of corn & turned back on account of the mud & then went ahunting and didn't see anything & John got me to help him skin a big bull up on the head of the Indian grave branch & Paw went down to the store & back & Bud & Poca started for home this morning & Jim Hant come back yet this makes five days out of his time
        for domestic 1^{00}

31 Tusday at Paws & worked on the kitchen all day & Poca came up & Bud to Reses she came to get a horse & Jim hant Come back yet & this makes six day that he has missed out of his time

spent during the month of December the sum of 15^{05}

1874

January 1874
1 Thirsday at Paw & me & Jim Clark up to Whites five mile below Waco & there stayed all nite

2 Friday at Whites five mile below Waco me & Jim Clark & we got aload of corn & came home at nite & Clark [illeg.] & in the

★ ★ ★

On January 3, 1874, Grandpa wrote in his diary that he "started for Bud" in Louisiana.
Cole Younger, often referred to as "Bud," went to Louisiana during the last part of December 1873. He was there through January 1874. (The Story of Cole Younger by Himself) *During that time the Shreveport and Hot Springs stagecoaches were robbed.*

★ ★ ★

nite me & Jim went to Masterville [illeg.] then to [illeg.] & there stayed all nite & from [illeg.] to marlin by 9 oclock the next morning & then taken the train for Hearne & I got aleter from home

3 Saturday morning at marlin & started for Bud from marlin to Hearne by rail $4^{00} & changed cars at Bremont & reached Hearne at 11 oclock & there had to lay over untill sunday nite at 8:30 & for Hotell Bill at Hearne

meals at Hearne	$4^{00}
for book & pencil	70

& exchanged $27.30 in coin for $30=00 in curency at marlin

4 Sunday at Hearne & had to lay over at Hearne untill 8:30 at nite & then taken the train for Palesteen

$	fair for Palesten by R.R.	$9^{80}
	for breakfast at Palesten	$1^{25}

& then taken the car for longview

5 Monday morning at Palesteen & taken the cars for longview & reached longview & twelve oclock

fare to longview by RR	$8.40
for diner at longview	$1.25
for ticket to Shrevesport	$6.80

& reached shreveport at 10 P.M. & then taken the Buss for the Boat

Buss fair $1.00
& taken the steamer for grantico
          fair on the boat to grantico $16.00
& stayed on the boat at shrevesport all nite

6 Tusday on board of the boat by the Emila labarge traveled all day on the boat & traveled about 150 mile by water

7 Wensday aboard of the steamer on Red River on the Emila Labard a st louis boat & sailed all day & passed a little town by the name of caushada & in the evening we landed at grantico & we hired a hack to take us to nachidoches & pad
          for hack from grantico to nachidoches   2^{00}
& we reached nachidoches at dark & put up the same house that Bud had put up at by the name of G. Fonteno & stayed all nite

8 Thirsday at nachidoches & remained there all day & we went & seen Jo [illeg.] & in the evening we setled our bill
          which was $4^{00}
          Stage fair from nachidoches to
          shresesport for me & Jim Snodgrass $18.00
& we left natchitoch at nine in the nite & traveled all nite on the stage & like to have froze to death

9 Friday morning at Daniel Comlandiers & taken breakfast at the Old Man House Pade him
          for Breakfast & [illeg.]   50
& then got on the stage & started for Mansfield & reached mansfield at nite & stayed there all nite & we still owe him for our nites lodging which was
          owe for nites lodging $3^{00}

10 Saturday morning in mansfield & then taken the stage for Shreveport & we went about 14 mile & came on to Bud in camp by the side of the road & we went on to S. Schalers & there taken a layover tickit & waited for Bud to get ready to go home we taken breakfast at S. Schalers & Bud he pad for it
          which was   40
& during the day Bud he sold his saddle bride & Boath of his ponies for $67^{50} in curency & me & Jim went to Hicory & stayed all day & at nite we went back to S. Schalers & stayed all nite

11 Sunday at S. Schalers & remained there all day & we got some little pins for to bring home & Bud he came & stayed all the rest of the time with us

12 Monday at S. Schalers & had to stay there all day & wait for the stage & we was apaying 75 cts(Prd) apease

13 Tusday at S. Schalers & setled our bill
which was 6^{00}
& we started for shrevesport & passed a little town by the name of Keecharge & then Shrevesport & reached Shrevesport at five A.M. & put up at the Planters Hotell
for lodging at the Hotell 5^{25}
for shaving three & cutting Jim hair 1^{25}

14 Wensday morning at Shrevesport & we taken the cars for Longview
for tickets 10^{20}
Breakfast at Longview 3^{00}
tickets to Hearne 26^{50}
& we traveled all day & reached Herne at 10 40 PM & put up at the Hotell

15 Thirsday morning at Hearne & had to lay over there all day & wait for the train & we taken the cars for Marlin at 6 ocl PM
tickits to Marlin 6^{00}
& changed cars at Bremet & reached marlin at 9 PM & put up the Hotell
for cutting hair & shave 1^{50}

16 Friday morning at Marlin & started for home
Hotell Bill 5^{00}
for hack for home 8^{00}
for gloves 1^{50}
Bud pade for shear 2^{00}
Snotgrass for shear 2^{75}
& we all reached home before nite & the man that Brought us out stayed at our house all nite

17 Saturday at Pa & the man that Brought us out started for home this morning & Bud he came up & Jim he went to Masterville this morning & back in the evening & Johney he came after him to go home & stay all nite

18 Sunday at Pa & in the morning Bill Wright he was here & I went with him to John Galaways & then I went to moreses & from there up to my place me & Old man Clark came up by my

field & then home & in the after noon I rote a leter home to T.W. Haun & Jim he went home last nite& back this evening & in the evening Bud, Poca, William Serena all came & stayed all nite

19 Monday at Pa & I went to Hatters & then to (dabenses), & back to masterville & mailed a letr to T.W.H. & I got home at nite & Bud, Poca, William & Serena is here all day & Bud & Poca they went home at nite & I poisened a wolf last nite & Clark came out to plow this morning

20 Tusday at Pa & me & Bill Maxey plowed all day & I poisoned a wolf last nite & dad & Serena went home this morning & Bud he came & stayed & made an ax handle Clark is aplowing today & Maxey girls came & stayed all day & Jim he was sick all day & at nite Bud & Bill Maxey they went down to the Sheltons to set up Jim he was sick all day & Bud let Snotgrass have his nely mar
for $100

21 Wensday at Pa & it is raining & old Clark he is fixed to go to Waco & it rained so that he didnt get to go & John he went to Masterville & Jim & Bill Maxey they plowed all day & in the evening I taken the pups & went ahunting & I shot at a der & Bud he cut poals for to fix his fence & there was to men here one to buy land & the other wanting to teach school & went from here to grigses

22 Thirsday at Pa & me & Jim & Bill Maxey they finished plow- ing & Bill he went home at nite & in the morning old Clark he went to Waco & after he left Charley he run off Charley Clark run off

23 Friday at Pa & me & Jim loaded to load of cotten & went to the Jin & stayed ther all nite

24 Saturday at Coals Jim & me & Jim we got home at noon & unloaded our seed & in the after noon me & John we went ahunting & John Goodman & mesilla was here & Thad he was here to and at nite he went home & Old Clark he got home from Waco & he give anah a pese of [illeg.]
for [illeg.] for anah by clark   --o-

Jim Maxey & Lue run off
25 Sunday at Pa & Jim he went home & Old Clark he went to Sheltons & in the evening Bud & John Galaway they came & to

men they came & stayed all nite & in the nite Jim & Lue they run
off & Bill Maxey he said that they went over on Elam me & John
Clark we went to Maxeys & to Sheltons at to oclock in the nite
to look fore them

26 Monday at Pa' & Maxey & Lue they run off last nite & i got
up the oxens this morning to go to halling cotten & Bud & Poca
they came & Bud he went to Masterville & old Clark he went to
Moreses & to Sheltons & Bud he got back at nite & he brought
me aletr from J.R. Heaton

27 Tusday at Pa & me & Bud we went down to the Jin & back
at nite & we worked the oxens & I seen the runaways at maxies
me & Bud halled aload of cotton apease & we sepered that we
had about 3 thousant or 32 hunderd weight & me & Jim halled
to load last friday which was about 3 thousand

28 Wensday at Pa & I halled wood all day & Thad & family they
came down at noon & Bud & Poca left here this morning &
Clark he seen maxey today & had a talk about the run off spree
& in the evening Jim Snotgrass he came up & I went to put out
stryctine & his horse got loose Thad & family is here to nite

29 Thirsday at Pa & in the evening me & Bud loaded to loads of
cotten & in the fore noon I went down to Dave's & there wasant
any of them home & I roat a leter to J.R. Heaton & sent it to the
office by Thad he went home this evening & his family stayed all
nite & Bud & Poca come up this morning & stayed all day & nite
& charley Shelton he was here & he brought aleter from Serena
lamenting the story of lue & Maxey & Tilman Bussby was here
today & him & Thad had some sort of asetlement

30 Friday at Pa & me & Bud we went to the jin & back & Bud
he stayed at maxies & left his load of seed there & Pa he went
home with Thad today & Old man Clark & wife went to moreses to nite & Bud & Poca is here to nite & the gal that came
down with Thad she stole aring & [illeg.] from mr Clark

31 [Missing]

February 1874
1 Sunday at Pa & Pa he is at Thads & it rained nearly all day &
I remained at the house all day & Dave vestal John Cunningham
Steward & another man was here John & Dave wanted to rent
land

2 Monday at Pa he is at Thads & I cut & split post untill noon
& then I done nothing & Mr Gipson he came after the dr
         & he pade me   75
that he owed me fore cuting hay & at nite me & John Clark we
went to moreses & there was a crowd there & we came home &
in the nite they sent after the Dr & I pened old [illeg.] she had a
calf

3 Tusday at Pa & Pa he is at Thads & I cut & split Post untill
noon & then I done nothing & Ellen & Vi washed all day & mrs
Clark she went to moreses & the Dr he went to gipsons to see
[illeg.] & Clarks horse died last nite & the old lady Clark stayed
at moreses all nite & at nite old Hatter he came & stayed all nite
& Paker & three other men came & stayed all nite & one of my
howns died last evening with stryctine

4 Wensday at Pa & Pa he is at Thads & Parker & three other men
left here this morning on the hunt of the man that killed the
pedler & old Hatter he is here yet & there was D [illeg.] died
with stryctine this morning & (dead) raysed in genral & me &
Ellen went to Moreses & stayed all day & back at nite & Bud he
went off with some men to hunt the man that killed the pedlor

5 Thirsday at Pa & Pa he is at Thads & it is araining this morning & I remained at the house all day & I done nothing & Gid
Gipsons child died this evening
                 G. Gipson

6 Friday at Pa&Pa he is at Thads & I went to Masterville & I got
me some Bluen & a comb & the dogs they followed me & they
didnt come back with me & Ben mores he died last nite & when
I came home they was just done diging his grave & John Clark
he pened 3 cows & calfs of Pa today & John Clark he went to
Peaves & got ahalf beef

7 Saturday at Pa & in the fore noon Thad he came & said that
Pa was sick & me & me went off there in the evening & John he
went after some beaf

10 Tusday at Thad & stayed there all day me & all the family &
William Serena & Poca & all nite & I set up half of the nite &
Old Clark he came up & stayed for diner

11 Wensday at Thads & me Ellen & Poca came home & the rest

of them stayed there & when we got to the spring branch we met old Clark he comenced on me & we had several words in the presents of Ellen & Poca & he went over to Masterville & we came on home & Mr Drake he came to see the oxens & me & him found them & he went home & at nite there was to men stayed all nite here & Shelton he came by & told what Old Clark said & in the evening i went to Dows & to moreses & Ben Galaway he was here to by the house & I blufed him

12 Thirsday at Pa & Pa he is at Thads & I went up there in the fore noon & back & when I got home Bud he was there & me Bud Poca & Ellen all went back to Thads in the evening for Pa he was taken worse in the nite last nite & I set up nearly all nite at Thads & old Clark he went to travs & stayed all nite [illeg.] nite I met him & on to Waco today

13 Friday at Thads & Pa is still low & all the children is there & we all remained there all day Bud Poca William Serena & in fact all the Youngers & in the evening Bud & Poca thcy went down home & at nite (Dave) Mixen & Bill Holcom they came & set up untill three & then went home

14 Saturday at Thads & Pa is still sick & Thad he Went down to Blackwells to get some potatoes for Pa & he got some & in the evening Almeda & Old Clark they came & Old Clark he brought Pa some things to eat 3 goblets of Jely onc small box of figs & Travis he came up at nite & went back home & Trav he said that he let Old Clark have 10 of Pa money got of [illeg.] $10 & almeda give Pa $350.75 that fred [illeg.] pade on the house that he got of Pa Trav said that he pade for the potatos that old Clark get he pad for potatos $3 & he got 17 [illeg.] which cost $4^{55} Old Clark he brought them to Pa

15 Sunday at Thads all the family & in the fore noon Paterson Bud [illeg.] father & Travis all came & in the evening Bud William & Serena & bety all went home & Hatter to & snotgrass he was here today Trav & Paterson & family all stayed all nite & I went to the store & got Pa a botle of brandy & Travis he is about half drunk

16 Monday at Thads & remained there all day & Pa is still low & Paterson & Bud they went home this morning & Trav to & in the fore noon Ben Galaway he was here to get the merida Wright

house & the old Pedler to & pade the pedler what me & Pa boath
owed him which was to dolars apease $4^{00}
& I got ma to hankercheifs & one apron which cost   75
& I let mily have ahalf dolar of Pa money to by to aprons & at
nite i set nearly all nite & we all have bin at Thads evry
since Pa taken sick
                    for stockens for Ellen of Ped   50

17 Tusday at Thads & remained there all day onley me & I went
home & robed a beagum to get some honey for Pa & I got back
by one & almeda she is at Thads yet & Bud & the rest of the
wagons is gone to the jin with the last of the cotton today &
Wood wife is at Old Clarks to day & dad he is gone to his dads
& he road my horse serene & Poca is at our house

18 Wensday at Thads me & all the family & we all remained
there all day & almeda she is here yet & I set up half of the nite
last nite & in the fore noon Bud Poca William & Serena they
came & they came in the buga & dad he road Buck Bud & Poca
they went back home in the evening William & Serena they
stayed & Tom Cox he came & stayed all nite & me & Ellen we
slept in the store
                    for Butens for Ellen   10
& Bob Crudep he came in the fore noon & back at nite

19 Thirsday at Thads me & all the family & we remained there
all day & all nite & I can't see as Pa is any better & Almeda she
is here yet & Ellen she went home with Rite & stayed all nit &
Trav he had one of his fits & they [illeg.]

20 Friday at Thads me & all the family & almeda she is here yet
& remained here all day & I set up all nite & dad & Serena they
slept in the store last nite & it rained nearly all day & nite

21 Saturday at Thads me & all the family & William he went
home this morning & he road Buck & almeda she is here yet
Trav & Bud they went home this morning & in the evening
William he came back & it rained nearly all last nite & me &
Ellen slept in the store & Bob Crudep he came after almeda this
evening

22 Sunday at Thads & the hole family is here yet & Trav he came
& Bud he came in the afternoon & I give Bud 8 dolars to pay the
cotton pickers (Abner) $5 Tilds $175 mr Green $125 & Almeda

she went home this morning & Bud he went back home this evening & Trav he went home this evening & J. Mixen & Bill Wilkerson they was here today & at nite dad & Serena they slept in the store & Tom Cox & to other men stayed here until 12 & then they went home & at super there was a general quarel [in code]

23 Monday at Thads me & all the family & we remained there all day & William he went home & he road Buck & Bud he came & went on to Waco & he taken my hide & the calf hide that belonged to Pa & I set up half of the nite & dad he stayed all nite

24   Died this morning at six ocl
Tusday at Thad's me & all the family & Pa he died this morning at six ocl & we sent for the to [illeg.] & they shaved him & me & them dressed him he had the best coat & pants that could be had any where & we sent & got the coffin Jim Cox he went after it Bob Moor he went with him & Travis he came in the morning & stayed all day & in the evening William & Old man Reid & wife they came & at nite Bud he came from Waco & he brought me thirty yards of calico which came to $3.7- & he sold a beef hide that he got $3.00 for & mary harden she came with Bud & after nite almeda & Paterson came & at 10 ocl cox & moor they came with the coffin & we put Pa in his coffin at half past eleven in the nite & Ellen she is at nixes & i went there & stayed all nite

25 Wensday at Thad's & the hole connections was here & they buried Pa at 11 oclock we all went to the burien but ma & Ellen & they were sick so that they couldnt Miss Yancy & Mrs Whatly they stayed with ma & Ellen while we went to the burien & almeda Paterson [illeg.] & wife mrs daten & nely they came to see me & Ellen Travis & Bety & Mary Harden they stayed here in the evening & Bud William Serena old man & wife all went down [illeg.] house to nite & there stayed all nite & in the evening gathered up all of Pa things & fixin to have them washed & in the evening there was a child buried near Pa grave

26 Thirsday at Thad & we all remained there all day & Old Clark & wife came & stayed until after diner & then they went back home he came in Pa buga & in the evening Rit & Mary Harden went down to Trav & stayed all nite & Trav he was drunk all day & nite & Harriet she came & washed all day & Tom Cox & wife had a fine girl

June 1874
1 Monday at home & I went to mr & mrs spenser & snotgrass
went on a horse hunt we went as far as (dobines) & there stayed
all nite & I taken my stray horses with me & lu hatter he came
to our camp that nite & in the evening me spenser & snotgrass
went to Hansfords heard

2 Tusday at dobines in camp me & Spenser & Snotgrass & we
packed up & started on to the Bosque & we hunted all day &
found nothing i& we camped at wins & a felow by the name of
Green claimed the stud & I let him have him

3 Wensday in camp at wins & we went out & pened the & IT
mars & we got another IT mar & one of the III mars & we
stayed at wins all nite again

4 Thirsday in camp at wins & we packed up for home & we
hunted the range as we come & we got several of our horses &
we stayed at ma all nite

5 Friday at ma & me & Spenser we helped snotgrass home with
his horses & the Ball Pony he got away from Spenser this morn-

★   ★   ★

*Grandpa had this intriguing rhyme
written in his diary:*
*When stemm and tryst
James L. Courtney is my h . . . .*
*[most of the last word appeared to have been
erased but I believe the word was "heist"].*
The definitions of the key words are:
* * stemm [stem]—a line of descendants
    from a particular ancestor*
* * tryst—a place of meeting, a prearranged
    meeting (variant pronunciation is with a
    long sound, which would rhyme with heist)*
* * heist—a robbery*
*   Could the rhyme mean that he stole the
name James L. Courtney?*

★   ★   ★

ing & I hunted some in the fore noon for him & in the after noon me spenser & Bob all hunted for him & couldnt find him & I raked [illeg.] in the morning & I had [illeg.] teeth cleaned this morning & pad

for pony cleaning 1⁰⁰

6 Saturday at ma & me & spenser & we hunted half of the day for the Ball Pony & we didnt find him & when we got back Threadgill he was here on the hunt of the Ball Pony & me & spenser we tryed to drive some bees & couldnt & we robed them

7 Sunday at ma & me & one of the young Threadgills hunted untill noon & I hunted all day for the Ball pony & didnt find him

8 Monday at ma & me & spenser densmore robed the bees in the fore noon & at nite me & him taken to [illeg.] to my house & sheltons [illeg.] they came & got [illeg.] colt he let them have it & Bud cuningham & several others went to Waco this morning

9 Tusday at ma & me & spenser went down to my house & we necked my cows together in the fore noon & in the after noon we done nothing & mrs Reese & family was here & she told me where scaball was & I went & got him in the evening & to of the yong Threadgills was here after the pony & I hadant found him

10 Wensday at ma & I hunted all around for ma horses & spenser he hunted for them & didnt find them & in the after noon me Ellen & Spenser all went down to dads & we stayed there all nite & me & Spenser & dad went afishing that nite & didnt get anything

11 Thirsday at dads me Ellen & spenser & we all went afishing & didnt ketch anything & we stayed there all day & nite

12 Friday at dads me Ellen & S. densman & we went down to the river afishing & we didant ketch anything only agar & we come back to dads & stayed all nite & Jim Parker he was at dads in the evening

13 Saturday at dads me Ellen & S densman & we packed up & came to ma we got there by noon & shelton & family they was there & malisa she has left ma & old clerk he is ashelling corn out of ma crips & in the evening me & Ellen we came home & malisa she came down & stayed awhile

14   cunningham mooved
Sunday at home & I sadled up & went up to ma & helped
spenser to [illeg.] to hack wheels & John Cunningham he is
mooving to my house this morning & ma & Spenser they taken
aride in the hack & I went with them to watleys & when we got
back me & spenser we went to look for our colts & didant find
them & we drove my R horse as we came & Bob he brought my
fily home this morning she is broke gentle & in the evening I
necked them together & turned them out

15 Monday at home & I went up to Richisons & back by noon
& it rained while I was gone & I seen boath of my mars the sorel
& Bay with the dun colt & cunningham he started to heard catle
this morning for cox

16 Tusday at home & cut briers in the morning & then threadgill he came after scaball this morning & I give [illeg.] & taken his
receipt for said horse & malisa she witnessed the receipt that he
give me & he promised to come on the [illeg.] of June to [illeg.]
the horse & cave Vestal & [illeg.] they was here today & I went
to ma & robed the beagum that belonged to me & Shelton & I
sold Wood a hide for 2.50 branded HK on hips

17 Wensday at home & I went up to ma & got some tools &
made a bedsted & then it rain the rest of the day & in the evening
I set out some pottoes & cabage plants & cuningham he came
home off of a cow hunt this evening

18 Thirsday at home & spenser he was here for breakfast & me
& him went down to stallsworth at noon & I posted the horse
                    & he charged me   6^{00}
for posting him & got home at nite & I brought a bond to have
filled the bond is for 75 dolars

19 Friday at home & I went ahunting in the morning & back by
Buds & Vestals & came home and made a gate against noon and
it rained some at noon & Mrs Vestal & saly eat diner here & in
the evening I went to Bud galaways & then to Old Johns & got
apar of bulet mols & Hix mores he was here after corn or money

20 Saturday at home & cut brush in the fore noon & William &
Serena Bob James Smith C. Rees & Bud all was here for diner &
Vi & Jo to & in the evening me James Smith & Tom Barron all
went ahunting & I killed a big buck & got home at dark & I
came by ma & Thad & family was there

21 Sunday at home & I cut up my Vinson & then me & Ellen went up to ma & Thad & family was there & dad & family & Eli & Eli & me ~ Ellen we went to ma & stayed all day & me & C Rees & Bob went up to the head of the creek after my mar & I got the gray & there was meeting here to nite White he preached & me & Ellen & Shelton & family stayed all nite at ma & Thad & family they went home this evening

22 Monday at ma & we went down home & then I came back up to ma & me & Spenser we went & made rails untill noon & I killed a little deer & in the after noon I went & looked for my fily & didant find [illeg.] & I grained my buck hide this evening & I killed a [illeg.] Just at nite a man he was over after my fily to run & John Cunningham he came home at dark

23 Tusday at home & I taken ma a pees of veneson & then me & Spenser we went to the bottom to make rails & I made 16 & I killed alitle 3 spike buck & we came home at noon & in the evening & grained a [illeg.] of my der hids & it rained a little to day & John he went back to the heard this morning & he returned home at dark & Wood he brought my hide back today

24 Wensday at home & me & Spenser we made rails part of the day & at noon the sheriff he came & somens me to apear at court in July to renew the bond as administrator & it rained at noon & Bill & Tom Barron came to us in the Botom & the sheff he came & taken John Erven & taken him to Marlin

25 Thirsday at home & I grained to deer hids this morning & Ellen she washed & John he went after his wagon & halled a load of wood in the fore noon & in the after noon I made some fence & then went ahunting & didant see anything

26 Friday at home & I went to the bottom & made 40 rails & then back home by noon & in the after noon smith & to of densman boys was here & gorge (Lepord) he was here to see John Cunningham & in the evening I went to Bobs after my little hown & they say that Jim Erven got home today from Marlin Jalle

27 Saturday at home and went ahunting with Willaman (Boby) & his to boys & we didant kill anything

28 Sunday at home & me & Ellen we went to ma & ma she was gone to Thads & I went to look for my dog & at nite we came

home & ma she come back from Thad at nite maxey he went with her

29 Monday at home & I went to ma & from there to Buds & then ahunting & back by ma & Trav he was there & ma & Bety they came down to my house & they stayed all day & smith Vestal & Bud & Ben Galaway they was here at my house & Spenser He is halling rails to fence the orchard so as to put the hogs in & me & Ellen we went up to ma & stayed all site & Milt Vestal he left here this evening & Old Clark he went to look for John

30 Tueday at ma & I made fence part of the day & in the evening we came down home & old Clark he came home from Patersons alooking for John

Spent during the month of June the sum of $7.50
& received the sum of 0^{00}

July 1874
1 Wensday at home & i went up to ma & made a fence awhile & then back home & I brought my beef home with me & I done nothing else all day & in the evening it rained a fine rain & John Clark he came back & one of the felows with him

2 Thirsday at home & I went Ahunting & didant kill anything & I taken anah up to ma & it rained to or three times today Bob Wideman & anerson they went ahunting with me & we went to Hosey gipsons while it was raining & seen Taylor at ma this morning & Bud he came to me this side of Reeses & in the evening Lis she raysed hell with the chickens & I had to moove them

3 Friday at home & I went up to ma & ground meat & then to the bottom & cut aset of logs for chicken coop

4 Saturday at home & went to ma & got the wagon & halled a load of wood & then plowed some & put out my potatoes & Bob Widaman was here & we went out & shot to der & cuningham shot at them & didant kill anything & John & Lisa they went to Widmans this evening

5 Sunday at home & hunted all day for to find out when I witnessed Dave Vestals deed & didant find it atall & me & Ellen eat

diner at milt Vestals & Dave Vestal he eat diner there to & John & Lisa came home this evening from Wedimans & Ellen Mrs Vestal & saly Mcabe all went up to ma this evening & doff Vestal he was here to get me to put his brand on record & I sold mrs Vestal a der hide & she let me have atub she charged me one dolar for the & I charged her one & fifty for the hide

6 Monday at home & fixed to go to Marlin & Saly Mcabe brought me some clothing to take to bob & I went up to ma & hitched up the hack & we went down as far as dads & Bud he come home to dads awhile after we got there & we stayed there all nite & in the evening me Bud & Dad all went afishing & I got some apels

7 Tusday at dads me ma Bud & the children & we all went to Marlin & Serena she went with us in the hack & I got ma these things

things for ma corsets	1^{00}
shews	1^{75}
nails	
starch	1^{00}
tobaco	10
bluen	75
gingam	25
coffe	35
pins	2^{00}
Butens	10
(geange)	25
tickits	25
& then for (g)	50
	50

& we stayed all day in town & ma let me have some money to pay my tax which was the amount of $8.55 & she let dad have the sum of $7.66 to pay his tax & I had a twenty changed for me this morning & in the evening we all come out to dads & stayed there all nite & Trav he was [illeg.] some today

8 Wensday at dads & me & Bud we cut out some timber to make & axle tree & then I hitched up & drove for home & we got home at noon & then I unloaded the things & then come on down home & then several [illeg.] Jim Erven & martha densman & saly mcabe & I brought Mr Vestal some things domestick calico [illeg.] & thread & in the evening I set out a lot of sweet potatos

9 Thirsday at home & me & Ellen we went up to ma & then me & Spenser we went & hunted for my horses untill noon & in the after noon I hunted by self & Spenser he went down to milts after some [illeg.] & this morning Taylor & Old man Jorden they was at ma & Taylor said that he intended to sell evry thing & Bob Widemans he helped Cuningham ho all day in his cotton & got up my horses to start to Waco in the morning

10 Friday at home & I fixed & started to Waco me & Spenser & I taken five horses to sell & Maxey & Lu they stayed all nite at ma last nite & we went on to Waco & it rained before we got there & when we got in town we seen Thad & Dave Mixen there aloading lumber & [illeg.] to & we stayed in town untill nite & then came out this side of town & camped for the nite & [illeg.] had a fine sun

11 Saturday in camp near Waco me & Spenser densman & we had 5 horses & we riged up & went back into town & stayed there untill noon & then we started for home & I to shirts for spenser which cost 80 cts & I got me some [illeg.] soda hooks & eyes & kneedles & I put up the gray mar at auction & they knocked her off at 18 dolars & I bid her in & we came back by coxs & stayed awhile & then on home & When I got to ma tomperson & dad was there & they had meeting there to nite

12 Sunday at home & doff Vestal he was here this morning & me & Ellen we went up to ma to meeting & Tompson he preached & we came home for diner & in the evening [illeg.] Poca & Mr Rees they came down & stayed awhile & I spoke to maxey to nite~at meeting & Sheltons child died this morning

13 Monday at home & me & Ellen we went up to ma & stayed all day & they buried sheltons child & we stayed at ma all day & for meeting at nite & Tompson he preached

14 Tusday at home & went up to ma & from there to mastervill & helped threash wheat all day for a man living on [illeg.] place & taylor he is using fidles today & he used him 3 days before 2 to marlin & yesterday & I went to Masterville & helped to thresh wheat all day

15 Wensday at Esters & helped to thresh wheat untill noon & then it rained so that we had to quit threshing for the day & I went down to Thads for diner & it is raining & thad he is gone

to Waco him & Dave & grays mashen is there by there wheat & Bill Scott he came to the thrashers this morning & he drove the rest of the time that we threshed & it rained in the evening so that we done nothing & I came home & I got some peaches out of Kinchlow orchard & Mr & Ellen we went up to ma to meeting & they had a fine time last nite old Clark & wife Bud Bill Maxey John Erven & Mary Edwards & lue & mrs mores & gilbert

16 Thirsday at nome & I went up to ma & then to masterville & helped to thrash wheat all day & at nite I stayed at Thad's & snotgrass he was heer at the mashene today & we all eat diner at Bonars & super to

17 Friday at Thads & I helped to thrash wheat at Bonars in the fore noon & in the after noon I helped to thrash at [illeg.] & Thad he went to Waco this morning & I went to cases & then down to Traves & stayed there for diner & the man left the mashene came & got it from Travis & then I came home & old Clark he worked Jack to Waco today

18 Saturday at home & I went ahunting & was gon all day & I seen Bob Wideman & Bob Johnes in the timber & I seen Dick Mculor to & we hunted all day & seen nothing & as I came home I seen manerva saly mcabc spenser Jim Vestal & frank densman at the hay as I came in & Jo Posey he came back to ma & stayed all nite

19 Sunday at home & me & Ellen we went up to ma for ma sent after us Jo Posey & gorge Clark came & then we went & stayed all day & White he preached in the evening!& Posey he is at ma yet

20 Monday at home & I howed all day & John Smaller & John Erven was here & I let John Erven have a der skin for miss mores & I let her have it for 15cts. & that pad for the chickens that I got of her & I got a botle of (worm) medisen of Mrs Vestal she owed me 25 cts & the botle setled all she owed me

21 Tusday at home & I went ahunting & came back by ma & old Clark Bud Jo Charley Clark & negro Bob they was all at ma & Bud & Part of the fellers was gathering horses for the sail & taylor he sent fidles home he has had him ever since we went to marlin the time we went & mrs Baker she was here this evening & I howed some & John Rite he was here

22 Wensday at home & I went after a cow on the range & then
I put up some post for the grape vine to run on & then I went up
to ma & got some peaches & Ellen she washed some this evening
& done nothing spenser he was here afixing mrs Vestals harnice
& Taylor & Old Clark & Bud & all his hands agathering horses
for the sail & me & Taylor & had quite a talk about the saile of
the stock & of the will

23 Thirsday at home & me & Ellen we went up to ma & then we
went to Thads & from there to Waco & we stayed at stons &
stayed all nite & I got my wheat that the fellers owed me at masterville & taken it & exchanged it for flour & I got me some coffee shugar & casteel soap & I got Ellen a pot & some calico

    all cost 1^{75}

    & I sold a der hide 1^{75}

& we stayed at stones all nite me & Ellen

24 Friday at stones & we hitched up & came to Travs for diner
& then come on down to ma & I got ma some coffee shugar casteel soap & to yards for the [illeg.] & then came on down home
& when we got home spenser densman he went with her & doff
densman & Hix mores was here this evening

25 Saturday at home & I went up to ma to the sail & I brought
3 horses Brown Dick & to to year old mares & rake & [illeg.]
double shovel plow & the old ax wagon then I went down home
& I taken my flour & I let hiram [illeg.] take one of the horses
that I bought to brake & at nite Thad & family & dad & family
they all came down to my house & stayed all nite

(<u>Items bought at sale — not readable;</u>
<u>written over it is</u>: old gordon robles watley bill Holcom refused
to go my security)

26 Sunday at home & me Ellen Thad family & dad & family we
all went up to ma & they all went over to Taylors but me Ellen &
dad & serene & [illeg.] reses was there

27 Monday to home & I went up to ma & me & Mr Reese we
made & axle tree for the wagon & put one coat of paint on it &
old Clark he sat around all day & ma she went down to [illeg.]
& stayed all day & Serena she went with her & serene she stayed
all nite at maxeys & ma she came home & Babe he came home
with me & stayed all nite & in the evening I cleaned out my
spring

28 Tusday at home & I went down to Mr Reeses & howed cotton all day for him to pay for his making the axle tree to ma
wagon & Rese he cut my hair this morning at ma & I come by
ma at dark & there by the name of (Batle) so they said & Mary
she left ma the day she whiped curk hefer she left

29 Wensday at home & I went out on the range & got back &
then I went up to ma & from there to Maxeys to see ma & from
there to coals & I got him to draw me to noats one to M.J.
Barron & the other to M.J. Barron & [illeg.] taylor administrator of the estate of T.H. Barron

first note for $59

& the last for 50^{50}

& then I left Coal & went down to snotgrasses for diner & then
me & snotgrass we went up to Jacksons store & then I went on
down to davisons & he went my security for $109.50 one to me
for 59 & the other for 50 0& then I came back to Snotgrasses &
stayed all nite & serene gorge Clark they went down to my house
& stayed all nite

30 Thirsday at snotgrasses & me & him we went to Jane
Guardeners & we got some peaches & I asked Jane to go my
security & to refused to do so & then I came on home & I came
by Gipsons & then there dad he came up last nite to ma & when
I got home saly mcable & to densmans boys & to moreses was
at my house & gorge Clark & I covered the pig pen in the
evening & cut the weeds from around the house & at nite me &
Ellen went up to ma & ma she is gon to Travs & saly mcabe she
eat diner here today & we stayed at ma all nite & old Clark he
went to Marlin with Batle this morning Jane Guardener he
refused to go my security

31 Friday at ma & ma is gon to Travs & I came down home in
the morning & tended to my things & then went back to ma &
cut peaches all day & frank & set galaway was there after some
peaches to eat & we stayed all nite at ma

Spent during the month of July the sum of 12^{85}
& received the sum of 0^{00}

August 1874
1 Saturday at ma & I went down home & tended to my things
& stoped ahole in the brush fence & got into a wasp nest & then
shortly afterward a very sharp pain in my back & legs so that I

could hardly walk & then went back [illeg.] to ma & then me Bud
Jo [illeg.] negros to all went to masterville & filled my note & then
I give Taylor my note for 59› & I bought 24 yards of morenas
which cost:

merenos 24 at 71½	$19.16
meat dish	51
shugar Boal	17
shugar boal	1.25
Pants	215

& then went down to Thads & we all came home ma she come
dad & family Taylor reses & charley & Bud we got home at nite
& me & Ellen stayed all nite at ma & dad & serene old Clark got
home from meeting this evening

2 Sunday & ma & I went down home in the morning & worked
on my [illeg.] untill noon & then went back up to ma & let saly
mcabe have my pony to ride up to & davy & Vi was there & dad
& Serena & Reses to boys & in the evening I let saly mcabe have
my pony to ride down home

3 Monday at ma & me & davy shelton doff Vestal dad ma & old
Mr Clark all went back to Thads to the sail & I bought ten yds
of bed ticking at fifteen cts per yard which

for bed ticking	1⁵⁰
for cambrick 5-1/5 at 13 cts for cambrick	71½
for 4 cards of hooks	27
flax thread 5 [illeg.]	25
for lamp	75
for 2 box colors	25
floss thread	32½

& in the evening i setled up & give my note for $26.56 & give
the to Bob Moor for security on my note haff & Tom Cox & Tom
Whaily refused to go my security & I got back to ma after dark
ma & the childrens didant come dad anah &old Mrs Clark come
back after dark & mex Jo worked on the fence at the house all
day for ma & Ellen she cut peaches all day at ma

4 Tusday at ma & I went home & then back to ma & dad he went
to masterville with the hack after ma & I fixed the mashene &
rake today & Eli he come this morning to ma cuningham John
Vestal was here after peaches & in the evening Bud Bill Maxey &
dad came from Masterville & I let Bill Maxey have-15 yds of
hook & eyes

merenos came to	$10^{72½}
hooks & eyes	20½
cambrick	35
	$11.28

at nite me & Ellen went down home & tomy he is sick

5 Wensday at home & me & John Cunningham went in the fore noon & got some mulbery timber to fill mr Bakers wagon & in the after noon I went up to ma & ground my ax & I seen maxey & I seen [illeg.] Paterson at ma today & another fellow with him & at nite Ellen she went up to ma to stay all nite for tomy he is sick & dad he went to coxes this morning after some canels & hant returned yet

6 Thirsday at home & me & John Cuningham worked on the wagon all day for Dave Vestal & there was some land buyers here today they had a fine par of Black horses & they went from here to Bob Widemans

8 Saturday at home & me & John Cunningham worked on Dave Vestals wagon all day we finished puting the spokes in & put the filows on one wheel & at noon I went up to ma & Bud & Maxey was there old Clark & family & ma she give anah a little tin plater & [illeg.] for me to bring to anah & at nite I went up to old Clarks cotton Patch & got some [illeg.] & ma said that Taylor said that I could have old John for my note for 39 dolars & at nite & drawn the note & roat a leter home to T.N.H.

9 Sunday at home & Mrs Baker & Mrs Mores was here for diner & Bob Wideman he came after diner & stayed awhile & he got Mr Moreses broad ax & in the evening Charley Reese & (H) Gipson came & Hiram he brought my [illeg.] home & at nite me & Ellen went up to ma to meeting & Ellen she stayed all nite at her ma & I came home & stayed by self

10 Monday at home & I necked Buck & the dun pony & drove them to ma & turned them loos & then I stayed at ma all day & cut peaches & Shelton & family was there & Spenser dad & family & thad in the evening & there was to men from Ellam & taken old Broad there names was Persell & they boath went my security for Old John & dad & Shelton & Serena all went to

Elam to the [illeg.] & back in the evening they went in ma hack & in the evening me & Ellen we came home & at dark dad & Serena they came & stayed all nite

11 Tusday at home & dad & Serena they was here & they went up to ma & me & Cuningham we worked on the wagon all day & there was a felow here for diner by the name of Palm

12 Wensday at home & me & Cuningham worked on the wagon all day we finished the wood work & three wheels by diner & in the evening we set the tires on the new wheeler& on the old ones & doff Vestal he helped us to set the tires & in the evening I went up to ma & got a sack of peaches

13 Thirsday at home & me & John Cuningham we finished Vestal wagon we made 3 new wheels [illeg.] couplen poals & set the other [illeg.] & in the evening ma spenser dad & Serena came down & stayed awhile & dad & Serena they stayed all night & ma & Spenser they went back & Anah she went home with them & at night I made to Par of hobels & shaved dad

14 Friday at home & I dressed four deer hide & made some hobels & dad & Serena they went up to ma this morning & Saly Mcabe was here this morning & Borowed [illeg.] & I went after my cows this morning & in the evening I went up to ma after anah & I got a peas of beef of cuningham

15 Saturday at home & I stayed at the nearley all day & in the evening I went up to ma & got some peaches & Borowed the canell moals & at nite me Bud dad Spenser Watley [illeg.] Taylor & Walls all went over to elam to meeting & we came away before meeting was over & it rained some at nite & Taylor he road Old John all day he road him to meeting

16 Sunday at home & I stayed at home nearly all day & Davy & Vi was here for dinner & in the evening they went to ma to meeting & they had meeting at the new house & Taylor he preached & I went back to ma & in the evening Poca she came home with me & stayed all nite & Taylor he used Old John to day came from meeting & ma dad & Serena all started for Waco this evening

17 Monday at home & Poca she is here & stayed all day & ma she is gone to Waco

18 Tusday at home & I went to Tom Coxes in the fore noon & I got some coffee

for coffee	1^{00}
for matches	25

& I left him 3 deer hids & 6 par of hotels for to sell for me hotels 25 cts apec & hids as folows one for 1 dolar & one for 150 & in the fore noon 250 all of the hids amount to 5 dolars & hobels come to 150 & in the evening me & John Cuningham we went out in the evening & killed one of my yearlings

19 Wensday at home & I went up to ma & me & Shelton we halled 3 loads of logs to build a chicken coop I

20 Thirsday at home & I taken anah up to ma & then after buck & the dun pony & then I came back to ma for diner & then me & dad we went out after Reb & Dads pony & then I necked reb & the dun pony together & turned them out & then I taken Buck home & saly mcabe & gorge clerk & ma & Jo was there

21 Friday at home & I started for Waco & I got to Waco in the evening & sold a der hide for 2.75 & mexican Jo he give some money to get Ellen some things

received	1^{50}

& I got some camphor gum

for camphor gum	15
for whiskey	75
for set of harnice	30.00

& Patterson went my security for the harnice

22 Saturday in camp on Bellside with Charly Reese & me & him come to Travs for breakfast & I got 3 pigs of Trav & then we came on to ma & Charley he went on home & I come on home & I left the pigs at ma & in the evening I went back to ma & got my pigs & I let Shelton have one

23 Sunday at home & I went down to coals & got my [illeg.] & then back to little Jo Jacksons & got some peaches & came on home me & Davy Huse

24 Monday at home & I hunted all day for my horses & didant find them & ma Shelton curk & to of sheltons children went to Travs this morning

25 Tusday at home & I hunted for my horses & I found the dun

on the (Hoolies)Branch & I pened him & road him & in the after
noon road the other & in the evening I traided the dun stud & a
cow & a calf for Old John I let Bud have the horse & cow & calf
for Old John & Shelton & Old Clark had a fuss this evening

26 Wensday at home & I hitched up Old John & Reb & then I
went up to ma & got the wagon & then went & got me a little
load of wood & taken the wagon up to ma by noon & in the after
noon I let Bob have my saddle to ride a mar for me & she bust-
ed it wide apart & I taken it home & riged it again & then sold
it to [illeg.] the next day

27 Thirsday at home & I went up to ma & Ellen she went to &
I cut a little Patch of hay & Bud started a horse hunting this
morning & I went to Dave in the evening to see him about the
cow & Batle is gathering his corn

28 Friday at home & I cut hay all day for doff vestal & I went up
to ma this morning & got the mashene

Borned

29 Saturday at home & I went up to ma & got the hack & taken
Ellen to her ma & then I went to cutting hay for Vestal & John
Cuningham & the children they came after me for Ellen she was
sick & at 12 oclock she give birth to a fine girl & in the evening
I went to Dave Vestals & Mrs Mores & Davy he brought me
some corn this evening & at nite I went down home & got a sack
of corn & then back up to ma & stayed all nite & Shelton & family is there Mr Shelton was with Ellen when the child was borned

30 Sunday at ma & Ellen is sick & I remained at the house untill
noon & Old Clark & his boys is gathering & halling cane all day
for Batle & in the evening I went down home & stayed awhile &
then went back up to ma & stayed all night there

31 Monday at ma & I stayed at the house untill noon & in the
evening I went up to Clarks Taffs galaways grisses Babes [illeg.]
Moreses & Bakers & then back to ma by nite & Bud came in off
of the horse hunt & I seen Ben Galaway this evening he just got
home

September 1874

1 Tusday at ma & I hunted all the morning for my horse & found
him near the house & I went down home & I got som coffe &

Shelton & family started home this morning!& Ben Galaway & Mr Grigs was here this morning

Spent during the month of August the sum of $2.15 & received the sum of $4.25

October 1874
24 Saturday at Elis [illeg.] & I went on into marlin & the witneses was all there Wood Broomfield hiram & the old man gibson & dad he went along with us to see what was done & the trial came off at 2 oc & the old [illeg.] & I had the cash to pay which was ten dolars & then we fixed & started home

for doll	10
for [illeg.]	25
for tools	60
for mending cycle[illeg.]	25

& William (Jorden) he bought the little gray mare of me this morning & he pade me five dolars
received of W. Jorden 5.00 $5^{00}
as part payment on the gray mar & me & Wood we came by Snotgrasses & stayed awhile & then we came on to my house & Wood he stayed all nite with me for Ellen she is at her ma

25 Sunday at home & I went up to ma to where Ellen was & I let wood have my pony to ride home this morning for his mare got away last nite for some (filder) left the bars down & I taken one of my horses & me & Jo went & got up my gray mar & in the evening I taken him to him & he pade me ten dolars in curency on the mar & he still ows me ten dolars & fifty cts in [illeg.] (missing) at Snotgrasses this evening I (missing) to Litle Rock Ark & I was at Coals and Jim Coxes & I seen Walls & in the evening I met Shelton and Josephene going to Sheltons & [illeg.] to me & Bud. (W) Taylor John Galaway & sons they was at ma & John Galaway he said that Peavy had gotton to old [illeg.] & wouldnt let him have her & he came on down here with me & I let him have the (instrament) of (W) that we had [illeg.] the catle to Proove that & [illeg.] [illeg.] when I sold to him
received of William Jordin in curency $10.00
as part payment on the little gray mar he ows me ten dol & fifty cts yet in [illeg.]

26 Monday at home & I hitched up & went to John (b) to cut ing hay & i got there at noon & in the after noon I cut hay for him & there was several there at work for him & a fellow by the name of (deck) & another fellow

27 Tusday at John (ber) (missing) hay all day for him & (missing) he came to where I was acuting & I cut all day & stayed at (b) all nite & there was several there Sam Ross & to other fellows & old mis (b) she brought me grapes from Mastervill that belonged to (c ker) & I went to Thads this morning & I sen Dave mixen there & miley

28 Wensday at (Bereses) & he pade me thirteen dolars this morning at part payment on the hay that I have cut for him
    received of JB 150 in curency
          250 coins $13^{00}
& cut hay all day for him & have cut him 18½ acers in all & I eat diner at [illeg.] & in the evening I came home & Thad he came to me this morning to where I was at work & I got to ma at nite & then I went down home at dark & saly mcabe she was there & then she went back up to Vestals & I brought Buds can of molases from [illeg.] this evening for him an the rake I

29 Thirsday at home & I went down to maxes & ground one cycle [illeg.] he turned for me & Bill he went to see [illeg.] & I came back by Daves & I got him to help me hall hay tomorrow & then I cut hay all day for myself & I got Shelton to rake this evening for me & at nite I went up to ma & got my wagon & to forks & I got some salt of ma & Bud & dad they came home from Waco this evening & dad he went on home & Bud he is at ma & there is a felow there to nite he is a [illeg.] & Bud said that Old Clark had indited me for carrying a pistol & Saly Mcabe she eat dinner here today

30 Friday at home & me Shelton & davy halled hay all day we halled five loads & in the evening Wood was here & davy he stayed untill after supper & then he went home & I went and staked my horses & I met Frank Densman as I came back

Spent during the month of October the sum of $41.55 & received the sum of $39.00

31 Saturday at home & I stayed at the house all day & worked on the hen house & in the evening davy he came & we toped off my hay stack & covered the hen house

November 1874
1 Sunday at home & I went down to smiths & got ten dolars that W. Jordain had left there for me as part pay for the gray mar

received of W Jordain 10 in curency 10^{00}
received of (C G B) 1.25 in curency 1^{25}
& I stayed at smith's for diner & Mrs Boid was there & I came on back by Stevensons & reeses & then on home & when I got home davy he was there & in the evening me & Ellen we went up to doff Vestals & they was fixing to moove & Ellen she got some onions of Mrs Vestal

2 Monday at home & I went & looked for my horses & didant find them I was at ma ahunting for them & then I came on back home & went down to maxes me & davy & ground my cycles & then I came back home & looked for my horses & didant find them & davy he was here for diner & in the evening I went ahunting & didant see anything & then I went & looked for my horses again & at nite I went & looked for my horses again & I found them up by the side of the Pastor & spenser densman he was here for supper & me & him put the chicken in the coop & then he went up to John Cuninghams & Bud he went to Marlin & he road Pady

3 Tusday at home & I cut davy Hughes 3 acer of grass & Wood & Gorge Williams was here to day & in the evening I went up to mcgees & ground my cycle & left the mashene at mcgees & came on home & got home at nite & Wood & davy is halling Dows hay this evening & Bud got home from Marlin this evening & Bud & Spenser is hunting Buds oxens

4 Wensday at home & I hitched up & went to mcgees & got the mashene & then went on up toward Taffs & met Anerson & me & him went on & I comenced to cutting hay for him & it looks so much like rain that I quit cutting hay for him & came on home & when I got home Jo Broomfield & Mcgees stepdaughters was here & malisa cuningham & they all stayed for diner & I went ahunting awhile & I went to where davy & Wood was halling hay & then up in the timber next to Taffs & the days they started a deer & run it off & I never seen it & I came back just at nite & Cuningham he was here this evening to get a stick of timber to make & axle tree for mrs mores & I met Hix moreses at the barn this evening & at nite Ellen & her to lady friends went over the crick to Broomfields & she left anah here with me & after dark I chained & tied my horses to a tree by my hay stack & taff he came to me today in the prarie while I was trying to cut hay for Anerson

5 Thirsday at home & I went over to Broomfields & I taken anah
with me for Ellen she stayed there last night & I cut hay awhile
& I broke the mashene & then I went over to [illeg.] & couldnt
fix it & I pade him for the work that he done before this time
which was one dolor

for Blacksmith wk $1^{00}

& then I came on back to Woods & borowed his sadle & me &
Ellen we came on home & then I went down to Jackson to the
Blacksmith shop & got the rod mended

for mending rod $50

pade Terel Jackson what I owed him which was   15

and then I came on back by mrs Bakers & Mrs Moreses & by
Dows & then home by nite & I let Cuningham have a stick of
timber to make an axle tree for mrs mores this morning & mcgee
he came to where I was cycle at this morning when I broke the
cycle driver rod

6 Friday at home & I went to W.F. Broomfields & cut him 3½
acers of grass & he raked it & I let him off for 3 acers & John
(b) he came here this morning before I started to cut hay & he
pade me what he owed me

received of John (b) in currency $10^{00}

& I eat diner at Woods today me & davy & I finished cutting hay
for him by to ocl & then I went home & I mete cuningham by
the side of the Estep field & I came on home & went to the
botem & got aload of Wood & I got home at nite my wood was
[illeg.] part of the old bee tree that me & davy cut

7 Saturday at home & I rized up & started for Waco & I stayed
at ma & then on to Waco & I pade for my stove & for the [illeg.]

22^{.65}$

for stove pade	$22^{65}
for [illeg.] the rest that was due Pade	8.50
for shews for anah pade	75
for candy pade	10
for cake pade	10
for matches pade	25
for english rum pade	25

& then I seen fred Hale & several others & at nite went out to
Patersons & stayed all nite & there was several others & I stayed
all nite & mary Bancorf was at Patersons

8 Sunday at Patersons & I started for home & John Paterson &
mary Bancorf came down to Travs & I give almeda a piece of

gum to make some [illeg.] & I came on down to Travs & stayed
for diner & he went out & seen old Clark for me & I done nothing & I eat diner at Travs & John Paterson mary bancorf farley
& old mrs Clark & after diner Jeff [illeg.] wife she came & stayed
awhile & then I came on home I stayed at ma & Bud Poca
Serena Shelton & family was all there & they wouldnt let me
have there wagon bed to go to marlin in & I came on down home
& then went over to Woods & from there to D. mcgees he pade
1 dolar

received of D Mcgee $1.00

& I borrowed the cutchman sadle & then I taken Wood sadle
home & then came on back & at dark there was to men came
here & stayed all nite one by the name of [illeg.] & the other by
the name of Clock they wanted some hay cut & doff Vestal came
& got his last [illeg.] of [illeg.] this evening

9 Monday at home & there was to men left here this morning
they stayed here all nite & me & Ellen went up to ma & then I
went on to Marlin & I seen Jim Snotgrass in (cap) [illeg.] office
& I made a contract with him for him to defend my case that old
Clark had accused me of carrying a pistol & I seen [illeg.] & B
issac Wright & in fact lots that I knew

for cake   20
tool   20

& then I came on to Old Man Reids & walls was there & Bud
dad & Snotgrass they all came there & stayed all nite & I left
marlin at abot ½ our by sun & crossed the bridge at dark

10 Tusday at old man reids me Bud dad Walls & Jim Snotgrass
& me Bud dad & Snotgrass all came home & Jim he stayed at
[illeg.] & we came on & stayed at old mis rites & then on up by
Buds & he stayed at home & dad he stayed at Bill Bits & I came
on to Dows & talked to him awhile & then on home & nobody
at home & I caught the pony & started for ma after Ellen & I
met her & Serena acoming & we all came on home & then
Serena she went back to ma & Ellen she got diner & then I went
to maxes & ground my cycle & he turned for me & old m reid
she give me some potatoes for anah & Ellen this morning & at
diner Davy he came & stayed awhile & in the evening I went
down to maxes & ground my cycle jim Maxey & Bud turned for
me while I ground the cycle

11 Wednesday at home & I went & cut hay for Raff Anerson all
day & I broke one of the sextons out of one of cycles & Jones he

came to where I was at work & taff he was there to & to other
fellows & I met Sam conley as I went Up there & John Cuningham he helped me to top my haystack this morning & when I
came home from cutting hay this evening Davy & Vi was here &
they stayed all nite & Mrs Baker she was here when I got home
& they stayed all nite & mrs Baker she was here when I got home
& she went up to Cuninghams & stayed all nite & Mr Jones he
was here this morning wanting hay cut

12 Thirsday at home & davy & Vi is here & I hired davy to rake
for me & me & him went to maxes & ground the cycles & Bud
& Spenser densman came by there while we was there & then we
came on back & negro bob he came on & overtaken us & he
pade me what he owed me

received   25

& I came on home & went on to cutting hay & I cut 3 rounds &
broke the cycle [illeg.] & me Jones he came to me & he came on
home with me & I loned him ma pitchforks & then I borowed
cuninghams saddle & went to get the rod mended & seen Terel
Jackson Buss [illeg.] Sam Jackson John Jordain & then went to
gorge [illeg.] & he mended the rod for me he charged me the
sum of 25 cts

for mending spent   25

& then I come on home & I seen to of the rits [illeg.] & I seen
Serena & one of the [illeg.] [illeg.] & I eat diner at Buds today
& Spenser he was there Mr Reid died today at [illeg.] on [illeg.]
place

13 Friday at home & I went up to Taff & cut hay for Jones & he
brought my diner to me & Jones & Taff they came to where I was
& I cut Jones 25 acers & I cut [illeg.] 1 acer & he pade me
($125) & then I went & comenced cutting Taffs hay & me &
davy we went to Jones for diner & Davy he raked all day for me
& at nite I went to Taffs & stayed all nite & davy he went home

14 Saturday at Raffs & I stayed there all nite & I ground my
cycles & then cut the rest of Taffs hay & davy he raked part of
the day for me & me & davy we came home at noon & davy he
stayed untill diner & then he went home & Jones he pade me $3
for cutting hay(his hay) & the [illeg.] acers that I cut for Taff he
give me &[illeg.] an davy for 10 dolars & at nite me & Ellen we
went up to ma to meeting & Ellen she stayed at her ma & I came
on home & Parson Tompsen he preached to nite & is at ma to
nite & I seen Walls at ma to nite & Bud he give me abill of sail

to give to William Gordain & he also give me & order to him for
some money he said it was 16 dol & Mrs Mores she paid me
what She owed me to nite

       received of Mrs Mores $3^{00}

& after meeting I came down home & stayed all nite by my self
& davy said that Mr. Reid died day before yesterday Bud said the
old mar give [illeg.] & it rained some tonite while wewas at
church & I witnessed a bill of sail from R.C. Barron to William
Gorden & William Maxey he was the other witness

15 Sunday at home & Ellen she stayed at her ma last nite & me
& Cuningham taken [illeg.] this morning & I borowed his sadle
& I went over to Mr Gordains & I give him the bill of sail from
Bud & I showed him the order that Bud give me to gordain for
Sixteen dollors & he said that he hadnt the money & he didant
know when he would have it & I came back home & I found
Buck on Pan Creek & I ran him to Mrs Moreses & there caught
him & I eat diner there & [illeg.] he was there for diner & to of
the densman boys Frank & Dolf & then I went over by Mrs
Bakers & she paid me coin part that she owed me

       received of Mrs Baker coin   500

& then I went down by maxes & then I borowed [illeg.] to
[illeg.] the pony home & I sent Gordains [illeg.] home by his
darkey & I came up by ma & then on down home davy he was
& then I went back up to ma & I taken the pony-for Ellen to ride
home & anah she is sick & we got home just as the rain came &
it rained all nite Spenser & (quilen) was at ma & all of shelton
folks (W) Taylor

16 Monday at home & I went to Marlin I went by mrs Bakers &
Buds & Jim Snotgrass & then by Old Man Reids & from there
to Marlin and I paid my tax

paid	$10.57
for toal	20
for cakes	25
for whiskey	75
for lard oil	50

& I went in & seen (o) & Rhymes & I told them to [illeg.] the
thing if they could & I seen the [illeg.] Elam & they put off the
tryal until saturday week & then I started for home & I got home
at about 10 or 11 ock in the nite & Ellen she was at cuninghams
& I went up there & brought anah home she is sick & she has
been evry since saturday & paid D.H. Hays tax for him it was

$3.55 he sent the money by me part of it by me and order to pid-cacke for the rest

17 Tusday at home & I went up to ma & I went & I went & drove up my yearlin & me & Shelton we killed it & I eat dinner at ma & there was a sick man eat diner there the felow [illeg.] & there was to felows came to me & Shelton while we were killing the beef one hunting horses & the other lived at [illeg.] he was riding a mule & then Shelton he brought me beaf down home for me & I borowed some salt of ma & she let him have some bees wax & we made a wax [illeg.] this evening me & Ellen & Martha Densman & davy & Jim they came awhile we was at work at the [illeg.] & they stayed all nite & martha she went up to cuning-hams & I let cuningham have one qr of beaf the front qr & in the evening I went after Dr Mcgee for anah she is sick & he came & give her 5 doses of medisin & some [illeg.] in [illeg.] & I give Davy his tax recepe to nite & the rest of the money that was due him

18 Wensday at home & I stayed at the house all day for Anna was sick all day & malisa she was here & Dave Vestal he brought his wagon over for John to make him a bed & they worked nearly all day in the rain & it rained all day

19 Thirsday at home & it is very cold & I stayed at the house all day for Anna she is sick & in the evening I went up to ma to get a bucket of milk & some buter for anna & I helped shelton fix [illeg.] in his wagon & then I came on home & stayed at home the rest of the day & malisa she was here today & old Clark he came over to ma while I was there & (quilen) he was there & Shelton & family & Shelton said that Dr McGee had taken his tB cow or at least the [illeg.]

20 Friday at home & I went down to Dan Coals mill & i bought 2 bu of meal of him

for meal of Coal	$1^{50}
for kneedls	10

& there were several there Bud John Rite Cuningham to [illeg.] & several other & I met Walls & Cooper and went down this side of Jacksons & I seen Hix Mores & Dolf Densman amaking rails in the bottom between Dows & maxes & Bud said that they were to go on the Estep field & I seen in the bottom as I came [illeg.] aload of wood

21 Saturday at home & I went ahunting in the fore noon & I killed a little yearling Buck up by Woods & then I came on home & I give cuningham one fore qr & in the after noon I cut up the meat & built a smoke in it & then I went ahunting down by Reses & I run some deer down by Gid Gipsons & up by the salt branch spring & I see that Old Clark has got acamp there & he has broke some prairie & mooved the old pen on this side of the branch & I came on back by Reses & Bud he was there & I talked awhile to them & then came on up the branch & then on home & I plated me a rawhide roap to nite after dark

22 Sunday at home & I stayed at home all day & I scalded the beef & put it out to dry & malisa she was herelawhile this morning & I paid them the meal that I owed cuningham

23 Monday at home & there was a felow here this morning from Henry Whits & said that White wanted some hay cut & I hitched up & went & cut him 3 acers of grass & there was several came to me to day Walter Canterbury Devers & to other felows & then I came on down by Clarks & Taff & Sparks & theywas there & Sparks he came on apeas with me & showed me where to cut his hay & then I came on home & Ellen she said that Manerva Vestal was here today

24 Tusday at home & I went over to ma & got davy to rake hay for me & he raked all day & he went with me to maxes & we ground the cycles then I came on & went& cut Sparks 4 acers of grass & me & Davy we went to Clarks for diner & there was a felow from Whits this morning wanting more hay cut & Bud Dobins Hix Mores & John Guardner came by where we were at work & Hix he bought me to letter one from home & the other from H.S. Crow & I sent by Wood for a sack of salt & I give him 3 dolars to get it with at nite I came home & Davy he came with me & stayed all nite with us & BUd he came & got his [illeg.] today I taken it off him & dobins & some felow set the prarie afire [illeg.] mcgees me davy & Sparks & Clark all seen the fire

25 Wensday at home & davy Huse he stayed here last nite & me & him went & cut & raked hay for Sparks all day I cut 6 acers for him & we went to Clarks for diner & Clark he was helping Taff kill hogs & in the after noon Clark & Sparks they halled hay & davy he came by & stayed untill super & then went on home & Wood & Dr. McGee came to where I was at work & Ellen said that Sheltons was here today & said that he was going to Marlin

26 Thirsday at home & I went to mrs moreses & then me & davy we went down to maxes to grind the cycles & they wouldant let me grind & then we went back to mrs moreses & we ground them there & came on (missing) Sparks Hay & then I went & cut one acer for Dolf Densman & me & Davy eat diner at my house today & then I went & cut some for Henry White & Davy he went to Elliots & I came home at nite & davy he came with me & then he went on home & saly mcabe she was at mrs moreses this morning & martha densman to & I wrote alleter to H.S. Crow to nite

27 Friday at home & I went & cut hay for Henry White & I cut him 3\ acers & Dave Vestal Hix Mores & Dolf Densman came by where I was at work & davy he raked for me & they fetched us some diner about 2 ocl & they was [illeg.] hay where we left & me & Davy we came by mcgees & ground the cycls & then we came on & davy he taken the rake up to the corner of ma pasture & I came on home with the mashine & Davy he went on home & Devers he came [illeg.] today & [illeg.] Dobins & ma she got home from Marlin this evening Maxey Jim went with her

28 Saturday at home & I went up to ma & helped Shelton to kill a hog & he give me the back bone & old [illeg.] the old [illeg.] man & quilen & Parson Skilens was there & then I came on back home & in the evening Ellen she got mrs Baker & malisa to help her make her mereno drapes & they finished it by bed time & I told Mrs Baker that Dolf Densman could come here & stay while he was going to school & cuningham he came home [illeg.] & at nite I went up to ma & stayed at the house untill meeting was over & then I give Shelton three leters one to H.S. Crow one to T.N. Haun & the other to Esq Ealern

29 Sunday at home & ma John Clark they came down here & stayed awhile & Ellen she went home with ma & mrs Baker she was here this morning & Davy he was here ahunting his horses & Shelton he started for Marlin this morning so ma said & after ma & Ellen left I fixed up& went up to Johns & then up to ma & they was all gone to meeting & I went in the house & stayed there untill meeting was over & me & Ellen stay there untill in the evening & there was several there Bees & family Walls Cooper gid Hosey & old Mrs Gipson all at ma for diner & in the evening grigs he came & Ellen she rode this pony down home & then he went on home

Dolf Densman

30 Monday at home & I went up to ma & Taylor he was there & I went over & seen steward & he said that he didant owe Walls anything & then I borowed 2 cups of coffee of ma & then came on home & cuningham he killed one of his [illeg.] & then I went to cutting hay & cut hay all day for myself & davy he raked in the after noon & Bud he came to me in the after noon & I give his $3.50 to get me a sack of salt & davy he stayed all nite & little Dolf Densman he came after dark he came to stay all nite & little Dolf came to go to school & mcgee he came to me today this evening

Spent during the month of November the sum of $48.25
& received the sum of $39.60
Spent up to the last of november $237.85 & received the sum of $189.30

December 1874
1 Tusday at home & davy & doff was here & I went & cut hay all day & davy he raked all day & in the evening I went up to Clarks & got the pitchforks & Wood he came to me & davy this morning & he brought the [illeg.] & Clark he didant bring the forks I had to go after them & davy he went home this evening

2 Wensday at home & I halled hay all day & Davy Huse & John Cuningham helped me hall all day & Clark he come to where we was at work & one of the Taffs boys was here after my dogs to run a panther so he said & Ellen she went up to her ma this evening & doff he come back with her & Davy he went home to nite & John Densman he was at John Cuninghams this evening & Ellen she brought me some coffe that Shelton fetched up from marlin for me & I give him the money and
                for coffee brought by Shelton $1.00
& Ellen she paid the coffe that I got of ma on Monday last

3 Thirsday at home & me Davy & John Cuningham halled one load of hay & John Rite he came just as we were finishing up the stack & then I went to cutting & Davy he rake & John & Hix they halled Johns hay & I let John have my wagon to hall on & in the evening I brought the mashene & rake down home & then I went up to ma & W. Taylor he was there & I got one & ½ bushel of salt of ma & a peice of beef & I drove old [illeg.] home & ma she give me the money that I let Bud have to get me a sack of salt & Davy he stayed all nite & Bud he killed a beef this day a heifer

4 Friday at home & I halled hay all day & Davy & Hix [illeg.] they helped me all day we halled 5 loads & Cuningham he went to mill & in the evening Frank Densman he came by with Dolf & Henry White he came to where we were halling hay & he paid me what he owed me

                    Reseived of Henry White $8.00

at nite it rained & Davy & Hix mores they stayed all nite

5 Saturday at home and I went to work and put up some fence around my hay and built hog pen and Davey and Hix went home this morning and it rained to day and Mrs Baker

6 Sunday at home and it rained all nite last nite and I was sicke and I went to McGee after some meddison and did not get it and I seen Wood skirting a beef and after I came home I chilled and Mrs Baker come down and got Cuningham to go after the Dr and he was not at home But he come at nit and he said that I had the neumony & he give me 4 powders & some drops & mrs Baker she stayed awhile & Dolf he came home this evening & Me & John taken a shave this morning Monday at home & I was sick all day & Mrs Baker she came & stayed awhile today & in the evening Davy he came & stayed awhile & Grigs & another man was here today wanting to exchange silver for gold the other man name was Joice so they said

8 Tusday at home & was sick all day & davy he came & halled me a load of wood & mrs Baker she was here to or 3 times today & [illeg.] & Charley Shelton he came down this evening Grigs child borned

9 Wensday at home & I was sick all day & I sent for the dr this morning & he came & he give me 5 powders & some turpentine & Bud he was here today & I let him have some shingle & he give me one dol for the

                    reseived for shing reseived $1.00

& he give anah 5 cts & mrs Baker she was here today & in the evening Unkle William & an came down & anah she went home with them & William & Serena they came & stayed [illeg.] awhile all nite Grigs her [illeg.] fine sun this evening

10 Thirsday at home & I was sick all day & ma she came down this morning & Charley Clark he drove the hack for her & dad & Serena they are here to & Bud & Davy they came & fenced my had for me & in the evening the Dr he came again & Cuning-

ham he had another fine sun this evening & mrs Baker she was here this evening & Hix Mores & after dark saly Mcabe she came awhile & ma & all the rest went home this evening & anah she went home with ma last nite

11 Friday at home & I was sick all day & dad & Serena they came by here this morning & then on home & anah she is at ma today & Poca she came & stayed awhile & dad & Serena they came by & she went on home & Mrs Baker she was here awhile & martha Densman & Bud he came by

12 Saturday at home & I was sick all day & Bud & Poca they came & Serena she was with them & Poca she stayed & Bud & Screna they went to mastervill & I give him $31.50 to get me some salt & Bud he taken ahide & sold for me branded as follows HK on side H on sholder & K on hip & got me some things for the hide

Sold one beef hide for	$2.00
for shugar	50
for tea	25
for soda	25
for one sack of salt	$3.50

& Bud he got back at dark & he brought me my salt & other things & they stayed for super & then him & Poca went on home Serena she stayed at Thads & Bud he give me back in money seventy five cts

13 Sunday at home & I was sick all day & manerva she was here awhile & martha Densman & Ellen she went to her ma this morning after anah & apiece of meat & doff he went to look for his pony

14 Monday at home & I was sick all day & I remained at the house all day & there wasant any one here doff he went to school & there wasant any school & he stayed at ma all day

15 Tusday at home & I went up to ma & taken her the salt that I owed her & I borowed ~ bushel of meal & then I went down to Buds & borowed his gun & he give me apiece of meat & then I came on home & it rained nearly all day & doff he didant go to school today & I stayed at the house the rest of the day I borowed Cuninghams sadle this morning to ride

16 Wensday at home & doff he went to school & Cuningham he

went down to see walls & I cleaned out my gun that I got of Bud
& then I went up to Clarks & back home & Clark [illeg.] sparks
was neither at home & in the after noon I went to hunt old
[illeg.] & was at ma & Davy & Vi was there & they killed one
hog today & then I went on to look for the cow & as I came on
home I seen a dead yearlin & I came on & fixed up some fence
as I came [illeg.] & doff he went to school this morning & got
his sadle

17 Thirsday at home & I stayed at the house all day & I cut some
brush & it rained part of the day & in the evening old [illeg.] she
came up & I went & pened her & me & Cuningham we killed a
little beef just at nite John he shot it & we got it skined just at dark

18 Friday at home & I went to mill & sent apeas of meat to ma
by doff & I taken Bud apeas of beef an I went to mill & stayed
at Buds awhile & then me & Bud we went on down to mill & the
woolfs got among moors sheep last nite & I got 2 bushel of meal

for meal 2 bu	$1.50
for fine comb	20
for caps	20

& I got some turnips of Dan Coal & then me & Bud came on up
to Litle Joes & we got some more turnips & I put the sack on Jim
Ervins wagon & me & Bud we came on & Merida Wright he
halled our meal as far as his house & then I stayed at Buds awhile
& Sally mcabe & John Densman was there & I came on home
without my turnips & I got home at nite & Dolf he said that the
sherif was at the schoolhouse after me today

19 Saturday at home & I went up to ma & taken the meal that I
owed her & Bud he came while was there & he went after the
Dr. for quilen & there was several grigs & several other &
Shelton he went to tend to quilens muls & then I came on & got
up my horses reb & Buck there was a preacher from Waco at ma
& doff he went over to Vestals this morning & I came on home
& stayed there the rest of the day & went up to Johns & he was
gon after his horses & [illeg.] & martha was there & I seen clerk
at ma this morning & he wants some hay cut for to make [illeg.]
for his sheep & mcgees dutchman was here this evening ahunting horses

21 Monday at home & I went up to ma & got my pig & my to
beagums & I seen moer there & then I came on home & eat
diner & then me & doff we went & halled a load of wood & at

nite moor came down & told me that they wouldant want any hay cut & at dark Shelton he came & he said that the sheref was after me & the offence was worse than the Jale & Shelton he went on home

22 Tusday at home & I taken anah & went up to ma & then to Buds & Clark & Sparks was at Buds & I went down to maxes & stayed & eat diner there & then went back up to Buds & me & Sparks we went over to Grays & then to [illeg.] & tompsons store then to Joneses & to Devers & then to J.L. Clarks & then at nite I went down to Woods & stayed all nite & I sold him one of my double shovels plows for six dolars he [illeg.] me the money

23 Wensday at Wood Broomfields & then went to Gordens & stayed untill after diner & the old man & Ed was there & Old man K he came there awhile & then I came on to ma & Ellen she was there & then I came on down home & fed the things & turned the calf loos & then got on my horse & went over to (rest of page missing)

1876

July 1876
5 Wensday at Cottners me & family & then me & Cotner & D. Taylor went on to Waco & got our grinding & then 3 mile this side of town & camped for the nite & Old Man Blackwell & Dow they went up with us & M Crowley he went to

6 Thirsday in camp 3 mile this side of Waco & we camp on to Cotners & stayed for diner & then on home & Cotner he give me the brand & shorts out of his wheat & he made a trade with me for me to make some bords & in the evening we came on home

7 Friday at home & I cut weeds out of my corn half of the day & in the evening it rained & me & Tom we looked for a bee tree & (rest of page torn off)

8 Saturday at home & me & Tom went to hunt for der or a bee tree all day & we eat diner at Bill Writs & we seen John Goodman & Old Man Write there & we seen J Write in the

botem & then we came on home by nite & Mr Lavender he went to Carolinas to church

9 Sunday at home & rod the sorel & went & drew up my horses & the sorel he fell back against the fence with me & then me & Ellen we went up to ma & stayed for diner & they organized a Sunday school ther today at the school house in the evening the Great H. [illeg.] the head of the temprance helled a temprance meeting at the said house & in the evening I went down in the botem & looked at the bate that I had out & then on home & I eat diner at Buds & Mr Write John Dulainy & Lackey

10 Monday at home & I plowed all day in my cotton patch north of the house & it is very hot & Mrs Lavender & Mr Bell & Henreta was here,

11 Tusday at home & howed in my corn untill noon & the negro Henry came & borowed twelve galons of flour for Bud & I howed in the afternoon & Mr Lavender & Mr Bell was here this evening

12 Wensday at home & I made a pig pen & then I went & got my to pigs that was at Bells & cut weeds in the yard the rest of the day & Ellen & mrs Lavender they went up to Bells last nite for ma she was sick & Bud he was here last nite & told us that ma was sick & I was at Buds & seen Jim & Su Dulany & Shelton at Buds

13 Thirsday at home & I cut weeds in my corn in the fore noon & Merida Write he was here & I loned him my wagon to go to Waco to.mill & in the evening I cut weeds & Mr Lavenders brother came to see him today

14 Friday at home & I cut weeds in my corn in the fore noon & in the after noon me & Tom Lavender we went ahunting and didant see anything & Ellen she went to D Vestals & stayed all day & Bud & Watson was here awhile today

15 Saturday at home & I stayed at the house nearly all day & in the evening I went up to ma & raked [illeg.] for ma & Mr Standridge & Mrs Smith was there & at nite we all went to hear Parson Tompson preach & S. Densman eat super here this evening & ma is sick

16 Sunday at home all day & Ellen & the children went to hear Tompson preach & Lavenders Brother started for home this morning & Mrs & Henreta Lavender went with him in the wagon

17 Monday at home & I went up to ma & then on to Cowbiau & I seen Mr Whatley & then on to Cotners and at Cotners we cut a tree in the fore noon & in the after noon we sawed this tree up

18 Tusday at Cotners & me & Cotner we cut & sawed bord timber all day & ma had a fine boy about 11 ocl in the day

19 Wensday at Cotners & I was here all day & Cotner he went up to the bosque to look for a cow

20 Thirsday at Cotners & I [illeg.] in the fore noon & in the afternoon I went up to Travs awhile & Babe he was there & then I went back to Cotners & me & him cut a tree in the evening & John Mixen & his tenant possed us in the creek & the crowd started up the country to look at the country

21 Friday at Cotners & we sawed timber in the fore noon & in the after noon I [illeg.] & old Mrs [illeg.] she was at Cotners for diner & we got some melons out of the field

22 Saturday at Cotners & me & Cotner & me & him went to masterville & we seen J. Blackwell as we went & we seen [illeg.] & the store at Masterville & hamp Threadgill & Old John Moor & then I came on to ma & there eat diner & ma said that the child was borned on the next day after I left that was on Tusday & Gilbert & Watson was here this evening

23 Sunday at home & Mr Gilbert he stayed here last nite & Mangrum he was at Lavenders this morning & we stayed at home all day

24 Monday at home & I cut some weeds in the fore noon & in the after noon done nothing & Bud he was here & me & Bud we went to McMayons & to Henry Whites & Bud he got a Pease of beef of White & we got Wat & Span he let m e have the hacknife for to stud that I taken him

25 Tusday at home & in the fore noon I went & looked for some bees with Tom Lavender & in the after noon I went to ma & Bud & Bell they was gone to mastervill & in the evening I killed one

of my little beefs branded HK on ribs & Bud he got me one pound of powder & to pound of salt

26 Wensday at Home & S Densman & Manerva Vestal & Martha T they was there & stayed all day & grigs he thrashed his wheat this morning & Henry he came & got the wagon for Bud to go to Waco & I was at Bud & Bells this morning & Bell & Bud & dad was here & John Shelton (rest of page torn off)

27 Thirsday at home & I went to Marlin with Mr Bell & we come back by a little after dark & I let Bud have [illeg.] to go to mill

28 Friday at home & Ellen & the children they went up to Bells & I stayed at home & I was at Bells this morning & Ellen she came home this evening & Bud he got home from Mill

29 Saturday at home & I went up to Buds & Jim Snotgrass he [illeg.] stayed at my house [rest of page unreadable]

September 1876
7 Thirsday at home & I worked on my seed (p   )

8 Friday at home & I made a basket in the fore noon & in the after noon I went down to D.F. Coals to mill & I got aload of my meal & no seed for Dan wasant at home & I got back by dark

9 Saturday at home & in the evening me & family went up to Cotners & stayed all nite & dad & Serena they was there Lavender is sick

10 Sunday at Cotners & T. (Bro) dad & Serena was there Bell & Vi & Lu they was there & we all come home at nite Lavender is sick

11 Monday at home & picked cotton part of the day & Bud he was here & got some timber to fix his wagon Lavender is very low

12 Tusday at home & picked cotton part of the day & Bud he was here & got some Timber to fix his wagon Lavender is very low

14 Thirsday at home & I went to the [illeg.] went in the wagon Dan Coal & D. Carey went with me in the wagon they tryed

Brother Dafen today & I taken to of my pigs to Buds this morning to the Butcher & I got a load- of cotton seed & I came back by ma & got some little things at nite & Uncle J. Shelton was at ma Lavender is very low

15 Friday at home & I covered my cotton seed pen in the fore noon & in the after noon I done nothing Lavender is very low

16 Saturday at home & I went ahunting & found a bee tree & Ellen she washed in the evening me & Ellen & the children went to cut the bee tree that I found & old man Lavender he is very low

17 Sunday at home & we stayed at home in the fore noon & in the afternoon me & family we went up to ma & stayed awhile & then back home & shelton & family was at ma & stayed awhile & then back home & Shelton he come to my house in the nite & stayed all nite he came to set up with Mr Lavender & there was plenty to set up with him there was G. Gipson J. White T.M. Grigs R.C. Barron & Mrs Shelton & old man Lavender is very low

18 Monday at home & I went ahunting awhile & then went & got my [illeg.] & I seen Mr H. White Seward [illeg.] & I met Dr. Watson & then got home by noon & in the after noon I picked cotton & Bud was here this morning & I borowed Mrs Lavenders sails at noon

Whits child died
19 Tusday at home & I stayed at Mr Lavenders all day with him for he is very low Mr Grigs John Watley was there & John Watley & Shelton & Reid stayed at my house to nite all nite White Child died today

20 Wensday at [illeg.] & stayed at Mrs Lavenders all day for Mr Lavender he died this morning about Sun Rise & me & Mr W Whatley we stayed at Mrs Lavenders in the fore part of the day & then me & Mr W Watley & R.C. Barron we went to the school house & made a cofin for mr Lavender & Reid he went to Durango after a cofin in the fore noon & didant get one & in the after noon he went to Troy after stuff to finish the coffin & Bud he went to Troy this morning after a par of pants & we got the coffin done by nite & put the corpse in at dark & dad & Serena they stayed all nite here

21 Thirsday at home & we buried Mr Lavender this morning about 10 or 11 ocl & the grass hoppers is thick here know & in the evening I went & got my horses & then went to Broomfields & got ten bushels of corn that he owed me & we setled about the beef that he got of me & I owe him three dolars & ten cts

22 Friday at home & me & Tom Lavender went to Buds & got our sows that we had there & then I went with him to look for there mar & I was at Cap Tompsons at twelve ocl & I was at Bells at nite after the children & Ellen & Lavenders women washed all day

23 Saturday at home & I picked cotton in the fore noon & Jim Dulainey he came & helped me pick cotton all day and at nite I went to Coals to mill & I seen D.F. Coal (Jep) Boid & Jim Bull & passed Buds this evening he was fixing his cow pen & I met Eli Seaguin as I went to mill & baby he overtaken me as I went to mill & I swaped my [illeg.]

24 Sunday at home & me & family went up to Bells & then I went to hear Mangrum preach & Tom Bures was there & we came back to Bells for diner & Bud & family was there & Reid & family & the two preachers & in the evening it rained a little & we came home at night & met Mcpherson this morning leading a horse

25 Monday at home & I went to Dan Jacksons & then hunted back home & I met George Dulaney & I met to of the boys going to Marlin with cotton

26 Tusday at home & Bud he came to my house this morning & wanted me to go & hall him a load of cotton to the Jin & I did so & he got it jined & Dan give me a load of seed & C. Rees he sent by me for some peaches 1 can

27 Wensday at home & i picked cotton all day & Tom he borowed Buck to hall a load of cotton from the field & henreta was here today

28 Thirsday at home & I picked cotton all day & Bud was here this evening to get me to hall a load of cotton to the jin & Fuller he was at Lavenders & Jim Steward he was there to

29 Friday at home & I halled a load of cotton for Bud to Coals

& I got back as far as Buds & I broke my wagon to of the felows & me & family stayed all nite at Buds borowed to dol of Bud to pay Jackson

30 Saturday at Buds & I fixed my wagon & then me & family came on home & then I washed for Ellen & in the evening me Bud & Bell went & killed a beef of Whits Bell went & seen him this morning the beef was branded [illeg.] on rite [illeg.] on the other paid Jackson 2 dol $2

Spent during the month of September the sum of $2.00 & received the sum of $2.00

October 1876
1 Sunday at home & me & Tom Lavender we went up to Buds & Bells & I got some beef & Tom he got some meal & then we came on back home

2 Monday at home & I went to Buds & Bells & then I went to Durango & then to all the Writs & Vestals Bakers & Mcphersons & then to Whitles & then back home & I got some coffe of Whatley

3 Tusday at home & I have a cotton picker today & Mr Grigs J. Dulainey Reid 3 of Sheltons T Lavender & Eli Smith & Bud & Poca & they picked all day for me they picked a wagon load of cotton & at nite Bud loaded a load of cotton for the jin of my cotton & we purpose to have [illeg.] here tonite

4 Wensday at home & me Bud T Lavender Bud Galaway we all went to D.F. Coles to the jin & we had to bale of cotton jined & we all came back to Buds & I stayed there all nite & I got a bushel of yelow cotton seed at the jin

5 Thirsday at Buds & I unloaded my cotton seed & then we came on home & Mr Grigs was here this morning & I shelled to bu of corn & then me Bud Tom started for Waco & we went with in three mils of the city & there camped for the nite & halled Buds to bale of cotton & he halled my bale

6 Friday at camp near Waco me T. Lavender W.J. Reid & R.C. Barron & we hitched up & drove into the city & we sold our cotton Tom got 8¾ Bud got 8¼ & I got 7¾ per pound & then we done our traiding & bought the folowing articles

coffe	$3.00
salt	1.75
flour	1.50
roap	50
matches	50
calico	1.80
cat flanen	90
one card butens	20
thread	50
diner	30
axle grease	20
shot	$1.45
soap	10
caps	25
melons	10
bread	25
corn	50
Breast Pin	2.00
R.C. Barron by cash	2.00
baging & ties	1.90
Pepper	20

& then hitched up & drove 5 miles & camped by Downes camp with Mike Elliet golden & graston & we seen McDaniel on the road as we went to Waco & Tom he boried [illeg.] dolors

7 Saturday at Downes in camp & then we hitched up & came on home & stayed at Cotners I paid mill $6.00 & then came on to the field & Jo he came out & we divided the [illeg.] & I brought my part home Bud he halled some [illeg.] his house & then I taken them on home & Ellen she is gone to grigses grigs came after her & I got home about 2 ocl in [illeg.] in & unloaded & then I went over to Grigses & brought Ellen & the Children home

8 Sunday at home & Bell & family was here for diner & [illeg.] John & Bill Watley to & Bud & the Old Dr Watson was here in the evening & I give ma fifty cts to have her picture taken
let ma have   50

9 Monday at home & I picked cotton in the fore noon & in the after noon I gathered a little load of corn & then I went up to Bells after Ellen & I taken him the salt that I owed him & Mrs Smith & Poca was at Bells & Lu she came down & stayed all nite & Tom Lavender he hall a load of cotton for mr Grigs & Dr Watson he was here this evening

10 Tusday at home & I helped mrs Lavender pick cotton all day
& Mr Grigs he helped untill noon & then his sister got worse &
they sent for him & Bells girls was here all day & at nite me &
mrs Lavender we went to Mr Grigses & stayed all nite with the
sick & they said that the sheriff came & taken McGee & put him
under bond for 500 dol

11 Wensday at mr Grigses me & Mrs Lavender & we came
home for breakfast & then I went & helped hall hay all day for
Bud & Bob Cox & Jim Dulainey was there & Poca & Lu they
came & stayed all day with Ellen & Poca she went back home in
the evening & I paid Bell $5.00 this morning & he give me D.F.
Coals note & T. Barron he was at Buds he is cutting hay for Bud
all day

Chapter 12

★　　★　　★

Fiddler's Green

GRANDPA DIED TWICE; that is, years before he actually died, his family thought he was dead. The whole family had gathered and were mourning their loss, or at least some of them were. Some of them couldn't wait to get their hands on his money. What none of them knew was that Grandpa could hear everything that was going on; he just couldn't move.

As Ida walked by she saw him move his little finger. He came out of his temporary paralysis and everything was fine. They didn't know what caused this to happen, and he had no lingering effects from the episode.

I can't imagine the horror of knowing that you were about to be buried alive. He apparently heard things he never forgot, because in later years he would be on his front porch looking over to the "little house" across the road and say to some of his grandchildren, "Look at them, just like buzzards waiting for me to die." (Grandpa built the little house for relatives who needed help to stay in. It was always full.)

Grandpa died on April 14, 1943, at Buie Clinic in Marlin, Texas. The doctor said he just wore out. Depending on which birthdate is correct (September 5, 1847 or October 31, 1846) he was ninety-five or ninety-six years old. He remained mentally alert and physically active until the very end. Even in his last year, when his legs had almost completely given out, he cut two cords of fire-wood while on his knees. His physical power was truly amazing. Relatives watched as he climbed a tall ladder at the age of ninety to shake a swarm of bees into a dishpan, covered them with a cloth, then descended the ladder and put the bees into a waiting hive.

My father was a pallbearer at Grandpa's funeral and said that although many people attended the services, some went straight to Grandpa's place to dig for treasure. It seems Grandpa was right about the buzzards.

★   ★   ★

According to Grandpa's will, he left Ollie a 160-acre farm in Haskell County and Ida 120 acres in Bell County and a house and lot in Belton. The farm in Blevins was to be divided by Lillie, Byron, Nettie's heirs, and Emma's heirs. Willie and Anna had been given land and advancements before Grandpa's death.

Byron was disappointed because he thought he should inherit the property in Blevins since he had lived with Grandpa for years after his wife was institutionalized. The will was contested but was eventually probated according to Grandpa's wishes.

Byron was said to have tried to buy out the other heirs' interest in the Blevins property, but legal fees had deteriorated the property's worth and the farm was sold.

Even though I wish the farm was still in the family, as it had been since a Mexican land grant was issued to my great-great-grandfather, Thomas Barron, the farmer who purchased it has really taken good care of it. Grandpa would be pleased.

★   ★   ★

Grandpa was no saint, nor was he a cold-blooded killer. He was a just man who fought against injustices done against his family and his beliefs.

Just as he wasn't afraid of living, he wasn't afraid of dying. He used to say he only had a few more years in this country and then he was going on over to Fiddler's Green. Fiddler's Green is a legendary resting place reserved just for cavalrymen. All of the dead troopers are said to be camping there with their friends.

Jesse James really lived life. He experienced more during his lifetime than the average person would in a hundred lifetimes. He took the good with the bad and never let the hand that life dealt him get him down. He just pulled himself up by his bootstraps and kept on going. A real fine man was gone forever when he took his final ride to Fiddler's Green.

Author's Note

I am still discovering new information about Grandpa every day. I sincerely hope I will find the rest of his diaries.

People disputing my claim may try to say that much of my evidence is only circumstantial. I actually have more concrete evidence proving who Jesse James really was than any other group, including the group led by James Ross and Betty Barr that claims Jesse James is in that questioned grave in Missouri. My evidence is as follows:

1. My photographs have been examined by experts in facial identification, and they all concluded that my family photographs match James family photographs. The Ross/Barr group and the James Farm use a portrait artist to authenticate their photographs.
2. The federal census record from 1850 shows that there was clearly no James L. Courtney listed as a child in the household of Stephen and Dianah Courtney. The 1860 federal census record shows that James L. Courtney suddenly appeared as the Courtneys' oldest child at the same age and time that Jesse left home.
3. A signature of "J. James" was written by my great-grandfather in his diary.

4. Documented evidence shows that the results and methods of the 1995 exhumation of the purported grave of Jesse James were very questionable. For example: misleading information reported by Starrs concerning the Missouri statutes governing exhumations; and the big question of where the tooth came from that was used by scientists for Mitochondrial DNA comparison tests against the MtDNA of the descendants of Jesse's sister.

5. There are historical reports that clearly contradict each other. For example: All reports about Jesse James stated that he didn't use tobacco, yet the teeth found in what has been reported to be the grave of Jesse James show otherwise. Another contradiction was Jesse's height. Many reports state he was 5'9 while other reports describe him as a tall man over 6'. If you read as many books about Jesse James as I have you will find that they are full of contradictory reports concerning his description.

6. I have evidence that many of the photographs that the Ross/Barr group and George Warfel claim as being authentic photographs of Jesse James are not him at all. This is evident in the book *The Many Faces of Jesse James* by Phillip Steele and George Warfel. Many of the photographs they claim are Jesse don't even match other photographs they claim are of Jesse James.

   The only photographs I agree are indeed photos of Jesse James are:
   • The most famous photo of Jesse James claimed to have been taken in Nebraksa in 1875. The Ross/ Barr group and I are in complete agreement on one issue: that the man in the most famous photograph of Jesse James is in fact him.
   • The photograph of Jesse James as a teenager claimed to have been taken in Jackson County, Missouri, in 1862.
   • The photograph of Jesse James as a Partisan Ranger (guerrilla) in his uniform.

7. Oral and written family history.

8. Numerous tales of buried treasure in my great-grandfather's yard.

9. His wealth—No other farmer in that area made that much money off of 160 acres of land.
10. He came from the same area in Missouri that Jesse James did.
11. My great-great-grandmother was missing an arm in the exact location that Zerelda was.
12. My great-great-grandmother is wearing a gown that is identical (proven by experts) to a gown Zerelda James Samuel is pictured wearing in a historically accepted photo.
13. Zerelda James Samuel's favorite flowers were said to be white carnations. My great-great-grandmother is wearing white carnations pinned to her dress in nearly every photograph I have of her.
14. White moles that Zerelda James Samuel had are said to be genetic. White moles run in my family.
15. Grandpa was the same age as Jesse James.
16. Grandpa was in many of the locations Jesse James was reported to have been.
17. Grandpa wrote in code frequently. The guerrilla group Jesse James rode with during the Civil War used coded messages.
18. Grandpa concealed the fingers of his left hand just as Jesse was said to do.
19. Bill Wilkerson, a known James Gang member, is mentioned in Grandpa's diary.
20. James Wilkerson, a known James Gang member, is listed in a federal census record as living in the household of Stephen and Dianah Courtney aka Andrew Jackson and Dianah Haun.
21. It has been written that Jesse was always in pain from his war wounds, especially the lung wound. Grandpa said he was never completely free of pain from injuries received during the Civil War. The doctor frequently gave him "powders" for his "pnumony."
22. Jesse James was said to have an eye problem where he would blink at different times; historians say it was from granulated eyelids. A lot of my relatives have the same blinking problem.

23. Jesse James was said to camp in a spot, then after dark he would move his camp a couple of miles in another direction. Grandpa wrote in his diary that he would camp and then move the camp to a different spot miles away after dark.

24. The Courtney connection to the James/Samuel family showing how Jesse came to use Courtney as his alias.

The above evidence is substantial. The photos speak for themselves. If others rebuff the evidence, it is beyond my control. But I know, in my heart, that my great-grandfather was indeed Jesse James.

* ★ ★

Bibliography

Baldwin, Margaret. *Wanted Frank & Jesse James: The Real Story.* New York: Messner, 1981.

Benet, William Rose. *The Reader's Encyclopedia,* 1965.

Brant, Marley. *Jesse James, The Man and the Myth.* Berkley: Berkley Publishing Group, 1998.

Bruns, Roger. *The Bandit Kings from Jesse James to Pretty Boy Floyd.* 1st ed. New York: Crown Publishers, 1995.

Croy, Homer. *Jesse James was my Neighbor.* New York: Duell, Sloan and Pearce, 1949.

Ernst, John. *Jesse James.* Englewood Cliffs, NJ: Prentice Hall, 1976.

"The Exhumation Begins," *The Kearney Courier,* July 1995.

Falls County (TX) Historical Commission. *Families of Falls County, Texas.* Austin, TX: Eakin, 1987.

Hamilton, John. *Jesse James: Heroes and Villains of the Wild West.* Edina, MN: Abdo & Daughters, c 1996.

Hansen, Ron. *The Assassination of Jesse James by the Coward Robert Ford.* 1st ed. New York: Knopf, 1983.

Harte, Bryce. *Missouri Creed.* New York: Berkley: Berkley Books, 1992.

"Hoaxers unimpressed," editorial, *The Kearney Courier,* July 1995.

James, Stella F. *In the Shadow of Jesse James.* Press A Division of Dragon Books, 1990.

"Jesse by Jehovah," *The Daily Gazette,* April 5, 1882.

McGrane, Martin Edward. *The Home of Jesse and Frank James, The James Farm.* SD: Caleb Perkins, 1994.

Montalbano, William D. "DNA links stone age skeleton to a modern man," *Austin American-Statesman,* March 9, 1997.

207

One Who Dares Not Now Disclose his Identity: The Life and Tragic Death of Jesse James. Utah: 1988.

"Probing a Mystery," *The Kearney Courier* "Special Collectors' Edition," 1996.

Ross, James R. *I, Jesse James.* Los Angeles: Dragon, 1988.

Settle, William A. Jr. *Jesse James Was His Name.* Columbia: University of Missouri Press, 1996.

Steele, Phillip W. *Jesse and Frank James: The Family History.* Gretna, LA: Pelican Pub., 1987.

Stiles, T. J. *Jesse James.* New York: Chelsea, 1994.

Stroh, Michael. DNA. The Pennstater, Internet (www.m2computers. com/indexa.html), 1997.

Triplett, Frank. *The Life, Times, and Treacherous Death of Jesse James.* New York: Promontory Press, 1970.

Time-Life Books, eds. *The Gunfighters.* Canada: Time, Inc., 1974.

The Life and Tragic Death of Jesse James, the Western Desperado. Austin, TX: Steck-Vaughn Co., 1966.

Vernon's Annotated Missouri Statutes. Disinterment. Section 214.205.

Film

"In Search of Jesse James," A&E Television Network, A&E Home Video, 1996.

"Jesse James—Legends of the American West," Cabin Fever Entertainment, 1992.

"The Life and Death of Jesse James," Casteel Productions.

Original Material

Courtney, James L. Personal diary. 1871–1876. In possession of Betty Duke.

To learn more about Jesse and Frank James, read *Noted Guerrillas* by John Newman Edwards. Shawnee, KS: Two Trails Publishing, 1877; Reprint 1996. (Edwards knew them personally.)

Betty Duke's findings about the real Jesse James are covered in an article by Anne Dingus in *Texas Monthly*, August 1997.